THE ART OF CAREER CHANGE

FOR INTROVERTS

THE ART OF CAREER CHANGE

FOR INTROVERTS

How to stop chasing the wrong jobs, utilise your strengths, and build your ideal career

Rebecca Healey, MBBS, MSc

Dedication

To my parents,

for always believing in me.

Table of Contents

Prologue

It was a particularly hot day, which would have been welcome were it not for the fact that the windows didn't open properly and there was no functional air conditioning. A single fan on a wobbly plastic stand churned away in the corner, sluggishly moving the warm, stale air around.

After a busy week, the end was finally in sight—just one more day to go. I didn't know anyone on my team and I'd never worked on this ward before. Typically at weekends, we junior doctors were shifted around to wherever was deemed necessary, by a rota coordinator we had never met. But it matters that team members know each other personally—for me, it makes all the difference.

So, the end of the week couldn't come soon enough. I was beyond tired.

I was just getting my bearings when a stern-faced staff nurse marched up to me. 'You the doc on this weekend?' she barked at my name badge.

She herself looked exhausted. The ward was seriously understaffed. I introduced myself. She looked again at my badge before thrusting a list of jobs into my hand as she went to answer the call bell. Over her shoulder, she said, 'By the way, there's no phlebs today, the PC's just crashed, and the bleep system's gone down.'

Phlebotomists are vital healthcare staff who take blood samples from patients each morning. Without them, it was all down to me. The online systems are vital in ordering all the tests we need and without them, we have no idea about the results. And the bleep system is the main way of contacting a more senior doctor should it be necessary. Things were shaping up well.

The ward phone was already ringing incessantly, but today there was no ward clerk to answer it. And neither I nor any of the nurses had the time to get to it. The jobs list detailed the sickest patients, the first of whom had a very low haemoglobin, which meant she was likely losing blood from somewhere and required a transfusion urgently. This required a blood test which would then be sent to the lab via the in-hospital pod system.

The patient was agitated, fed up, and frightened of needles. After applying every tactic I could think of to calm her down, including a long conversation about her family and a cup of tea and a biscuit, finally she agreed to let me take a sample. I inserted a cannula into her vein at the same time and bandaged it carefully. I labelled the sample and placed it in the pod as fast as I could, before realising that the pod system was broken too. The pod is a tube system that allows efficient transport of test samples directly to the hospital lab. I asked the nurse if anyone could take it to the lab for me, but I got the answer I expected. Not enough staff to leave the ward.

Exasperated, I ran down to the lab myself, secretly relieved to escape the stifling air on the ward, even if just for a few minutes. I got back just in time to witness my patient yanking the cannula clean out of her vein, agitated and angry all over again. At exactly the same moment, I was called away to a sicker gentleman and while I was there, a confused—but otherwise healthy—lady started screaming obscenities repetitively, upsetting the others in her bay. I looked around for assistance, but at that moment there was no other member of staff in sight. I'd never seen a ward so short-staffed.

I looked at the clock: 11 a.m. The pile of jobs had somehow grown while I wasn't looking, and the ward round had yet to take place. My spirits sank without trace and my head was pounding. My confidence was slipping away with every new job that added itself to the pile. I couldn't give anyone the time and care I knew they needed, and this broke my heart. There was no way I could do all this alone.

I fervently wished to be anywhere but here.

Which begged a rather important question.

How did I get here?

Chapter 1

Develop Self-Awareness

'Not until we are lost do we begin to understand ourselves.'

-HENRY DAVID THOREAU

Becoming self-aware involves a level of reflection difficult to achieve without leaving our comfort zone. Few people are truly aware of who they really are or what they want out of life. According to the work of organisational psychologist Tasha Eurich, although around 95 per cent of people may think they are self-aware, only 10–15 per cent of people truly are.[1] A large 2014 study of 22 meta-analyses, comprising over 357,000 people, backs this up.[2]

It sometimes takes a life-shattering event or serious illness to truly gain self-awareness. We are tested, taken out of our comfort zone, and forced to ask some important and difficult questions. It's tough going. But why wait for life to reach that stage? Why not start the process now, while there are so many life-enriching options still available to us, and while physical health still permits them? How much fulfilment could you be missing out on right now through lack of self-awareness?

We live in a highly-developed society. A large proportion of young adults now complete higher education and there are countless opportunities for lifelong learning online. It seems we can achieve anything. But, despite this progress and potential, it remains possible to meander through life without ever examining who we really are.

When considering changing role, job, or even career, it's easy to get swept up. The prospect of change is exciting and can be all-consuming. But I guarantee that taking a little extra time to get to know yourself now will save you time and energy later. It will give you clarity and allow you to make realistic plans. It will help prevent you from repeating past mistakes. Most importantly, it will force you to be honest in establishing what you want to do with your life. And in return, your chosen life will nurture your true self.

What makes me, me?

Personality is everything that makes us unique. It shapes our behaviours, feelings, thoughts, and relationships. It affects our perceptions of the world and of those around us. It shapes how other people react to us.

The American Psychological Association refers to personality as 'individual differences in characteristic patterns of thinking, feeling and behaving.'[3] In their book *Theories of Personality*, Feist and Feist tell us that, 'although no single definition is acceptable to all personality theorists, we can say that personality is a pattern of relatively permanent traits and unique characteristics that give both consistency and individuality to a person's behaviour.'[4] Carl Jung, the Swiss psychiatrist and father of analytical psychology, famously described it as, 'the supreme realisation of the innate idiosyncrasy of a living being. It is an act of high courage flung in the face of life, the absolute affirmation of all that constitutes the individual, the most successful adaptation to the universal conditions of existence coupled with the greatest possible freedom for self-determination.'[5]

Clearly, personality isn't easy to define. Psychologists do not share a universally accepted definition. Indeed, it has kept them fascinated for centuries. The first recorded personality model is thought to have been initiated over two thousand years ago by Hippocrates, the father of modern medicine.[6] It's a popular subject too—a simple Google search on the word 'personality' (at the time of writing) brings back around 665 *million* results.

It seems almost impossible to define what makes us unique. Perhaps that's a good thing. There's something comforting in being undefinable.

What we *do* know is that we're all different. We are more than just a series of traits and characteristics. One person's bliss may be another's nightmare. One person's notion of surviving and thriving could be another's notion of outright bullying. Some of us can instinctively gel with those around us while others may take years to form close relationships. You only need to take a look around you right now, to experience just one day of interaction with others, to realise how different we all are.

The introversion-extroversion spectrum

Our society tends to reward charismatic, assertive leaders, resulting in the widespread perception that introversion is an undesirable characteristic for general survival. As recently as 2010, via the *Diagnostic and Statistical Manual*[7] (the authoritative clinical guide to diagnosing mental illness) the American Psychiatric Association even considered classifying introverted personality as an actual *disorder*.

The word introvert may conjure up the image of a shy, retreating loner with little to say. Other widespread misperceptions include 'quiet', 'distant', 'elusive', 'detached', 'isolated' and even 'antisocial'.[8] But the introversion-extroversion spectrum has little to do with these labels. It centres on how we respond to external environmental stimuli, and how we choose to direct our energy in return. Extroverted individuals tend to be instinctively reactive to their immediate environment. They are more focused on the outside world and more energised by external stimulation, interacting readily with others. They are more likely to look outward to recharge their batteries, in such settings as social events or lively workplaces. Introverts, on the other hand, tend to instinctively look inwards in response to their environment. They think and analyse before reacting. They focus their energy on their inner world of ideas, thoughts, and feelings. They can become drained by external stimulation and tend to crave quieter spaces where they can reflect on their experiences and recharge.[9]

Despite the myriad means of describing introversion, all touch in some way on this notion of inward versus outward direction of energy.

Introversion is not as uncommon as you might think. Studies have shown that introverts may make up between 36 and 50 per cent of the general population.[10,11]

The stigma of introversion often makes us unwilling to reveal any introverted tendencies. The cultural bias towards extroversion may begin in the classroom, where children learn from an early age that they need to 'perform' to an extroverted ideal in their daily lives; they may instinctively mask their need for quiet and solitude. But these aren't necessarily traits that should be suppressed. Some of history's most influential thinkers and leaders are reported to have been introverts, including Albert Einstein, Mahatma Gandhi, and Eleanor Roosevelt.

Jung coined the terms 'introverted' and 'extroverted' in his seminal work, *Psychological Types*, originally published in 1921. He observed a pattern of fundamental differences in healthy people, based on their basic patterns of behaviour, which remained largely unchanged throughout their lives. He presented a model describing two ends of an introversion 'spectrum' and noted that 'each person seems to be energised more by either the external world (extroversion) or the internal world (introversion).'[12]

Those of us who require regular time alone in order to recharge, who reach a cut-off point after being in a group setting for too long, are likely to lean towards introversion. Being in large groups for long periods is an energy drain for introverts, and it can become exhausting. Conversely, those who feel energised by being around others are likely to possess mainly extroverted tendencies. Being alone for long periods is an energy drain for extroverts.

It was German psychologist Jans Eysenck that originally proposed a cause for this difference in energy. According to his work, the introversion-extroversion spectrum is caused by differences in levels of activity within the area of the brain involved in arousing consciousness—an area known as the *reticular activating system*. Introverted personalities have lower 'response thresholds' and as a consequence are more cortically-aroused than their extroverted counterparts. The model also predicted that at lower levels of brain stimulation, introverts would tend to outperform extroverts, and vice versa at levels of high stimulation. Eysenck later published results of behavioural studies that were consistent with his model.[13]

And in 2004, Eysenck's theory was proven scientifically.[14]

So, what does all this mean?

It may be that extroverts need to work harder to arouse their minds to a level at which they can function comfortably. This may explain why the same high-stimulation environments experienced as energising for extroverts can become almost intolerable for introverts.

Introversion and extroversion exist as a spectrum rather than as distinct personality types. Although we can exist anywhere along the spectrum, we're more likely to show a majority of either introverted or extroverted *preferences*—hence the terms 'introvert' and 'extrovert'. But no one is a complete extrovert or introvert; we all have a combination of both traits. We all need moderation and balance. An extrovert can still become drained after too much stimulation, just as an introvert can still feel isolated after too much time alone. It's what defines 'too much' that's different for different people. With this in mind, we'll use 'introvert' and 'extrovert' to describe those with *overall preferences* for introversion and extroversion respectively.

Do you have introverted personality characteristics?

Introverts need time and space to recharge. Recharging might involve getting away from the crowds, a quiet chat with a friend, or simply time alone to reflect.

Introverts can be highly sensitive. Not just in the emotional sense, but in terms of the entire neurological system. This means that such a person may tend to be more sensitive to certain sounds, smells, sights, and emotional cues than the average person. The 'Highly Sensitive Person' (HSP), a term coined by clinical psychologist Dr Elaine Aron, is thought to represent around 20 per cent of the general population, describing a person with this increased sensitivity of the central nervous system.[15]

Research suggests that 70 per cent of HSPs are also introverts.[16] According to Dr Aron, HSPs have greater depth of processing of external information and are much more prone to overwhelm and overstimulation, with extreme sensitivity to smells, sounds, and light. HSPs also tend to display greater emotional reactivity and empathy. Dr Aron and colleagues recently used functional MRI to demonstrate this,[17] observing that greater HSP scores were associated with increased activity in areas of the brain related to awareness, integration of sensory information, preparation for action, and empathy.

Introverts tend to dislike small talk. But that doesn't mean they don't like talking with others—quite the opposite. Introverts thrive on deep and meaningful conversations about big topics that matter to them. A one-to-one conversation on the meaning of life could hold an introvert captivated for hours. But twenty minutes of group banter can leave an introvert drained and frantically scanning for a polite escape.

Introverts are deep thinkers. They prefer to take the time to carefully consider their responses, decisions, and life in general. They need to think things through before taking action and are reluctant to speak up until they've considered the issues at hand. Consequently, they are often overlooked in group situations. Work meetings and professional networking events may be particularly challenging. Any situation involving pressure to think and react 'on tap' may drastically hamper performance. Autonomy and space are crucial.

Contrary to popular belief, introverts are skilled communicators and negotiators. They appreciate nuance and detail in language and expression, and they're far less direct in their communication than extroverts. In our extrovert-biased modern workplace culture, it's often the gregarious who shine and succeed. Image, charisma, and persuasiveness have too often outranked character and consistency, frequently to the overall detriment of organisational performance.

But quieter doesn't necessarily mean less effective. Introverts' communication may often be overlooked and unheard, but it is no less valuable. While extroverts tend to talk through their ideas directly as they arise, introverts prefer to think things through carefully before taking action. When they do speak, it is thoughtful and more likely to contribute substance to the discussion. Their tendency to avoid the limelight—and to take the time to ponder—makes them innate listeners. They will carefully consider the thoughts and opinions of others before making decisions. It's this capacity to listen with empathy and understand others that determines the ability to engage and communicate in a meaningful way.

Many people confuse introversion with shyness, but the two are completely different. The key differences centre on motivations, behaviours, and fear. Shy people tend to be more self-conscious around others, especially on first meeting. They may actively *fear* social interaction, which to them can be painful and stressful. Introverts, on the other hand, may feel perfectly comfortable around others, engaging with ease. But they are drained by it, so they simply have less motivation to do so.

For introverts, a quieter environment is simply more appealing.

Introverts are just as capable of engaging in social situations as extroverts, but they may need an equal amount of quiet time afterwards. That's not to say introverts don't need, or benefit, from interaction with others—on a one-on-one basis, introverts are likely to form deep and meaningful connections.

Introverts are good at relating to others. While socialising with many different people comes naturally to extroverts, introverts are more likely to develop closer one-to-one relationships, building up their networks slowly but surely. They are also more likely to consider the opinions and feelings of others when making decisions that affect a group, improving outcomes for all.[18] While the professional relationships they form may be fewer, they are more likely to be built on solid foundations.

Introversion determines the environment in which we feel most at peace and rejuvenated. It is the tendency to gravitate towards that peaceful and replenishing state, rather than a fear of interaction with others. Of course, an introverted person can be shy as well, as can an extrovert. Extroversion is not necessarily synonymous with innate social skills, nor introversion with a lack of them. It's just that, conceptually speaking, they are separate aspects of what makes up a personality.

The Myers Briggs Type Indicator (MBTI)

Since Jung, the field of psychology has exploded with new theories. The desire to categorize and explain the complexities of human behaviour with a convenient and complete model remains, and it has led to a number of theory-based personality tests. One of them, the Myers Briggs Type Indicator (MBTI), incorporates the introversion-extroversion spectrum. Its developers and authors were a mother/daughter duo, Katherine Cook Briggs and Isabel Briggs Myers[19] who were fascinated by Jung's ideas and wanted to help others understand themselves and those around them. The resulting definitive MBTI text, 'Gifts Differing', was completed a short time before Isabel's death in 1980.[20] Years later, the MBTI has become one of the world's most widely used tool for understanding personality differences.[21]

Interpretation of the MBTI

The questionnaire-based tool results in a combination of the following four preferences:

How you use your energy: If you prefer to deal with ideas, information, and beliefs ('the inner world'), then your inclination is towards *introversion* (I). If you would rather spend your time dealing with people and situations ('the outer world'), then your inclination is more towards *extroversion* (E).

How you process information: If you prefer to focus on the facts alone, then you have a preference for *sensing* (S). If you prefer to interpret that information—for example, by adding meaning to it or generating ideas from it—you are displaying a preference for *intuition* (N).

How you make decisions: If you like to make decisions objectively, pragmatically, and consistently, using logic, you have a preference for *thinking* (T). If you prefer to make decisions subjectively, based on your own values and beliefs, other people, and unique circumstances, you show a preference for *feeling* (F).

How you deal with the outside world: If you prefer your life to be organised and stable, adhering to plans, your preference is for *judging* (J). If you like to keep an open mind to new options, are flexible, and respond to new situations as they arise, you have a preference for *perception* (P).

The resulting four preferences lead to a four-letter combination, one of sixteen possible combinations, each of which is a personality type described in the Myers-Briggs model.

'Let him that would move the world first move himself.'

-SOCRATES

We may think we know ourselves, but our knowledge only stretches as far as the situations we put ourselves in and the people we spend our time with. If these situations consist of just routine home and work activities, can we ever really test our strengths and limits? Can we ever open our minds to new opportunities and ways of thinking?

It's easy to get stuck in a rut. We all have commitments. It seems simpler to push any angst to the back of our minds and deal with it later, when we have more time. But that time rarely appears. The familiar becomes comfortable, even if it's bad. So, perhaps it's time to discover what makes you thrive. After all, how can you know where to go from here if you don't know where you want to be?

Take yourself out of your comfort zone

This doesn't mean you need to sign up for the next available skydiving experience. It just means trying something you wouldn't normally do. Perhaps you could take up a new type of exercise or join a gym. Visit a local museum or gallery or nature reserve. Take a different route to work. Anything. It could be the tiniest of steps, but what matters is that you take it, because it will help open your eyes to the options available to you. In doing so, you can create small ripples of change that will eventually lead to something far greater. We spend so much of our working lives mixing only with similar people, from similar colleges or similar jobs. This narrows our world view and increases our risk of developing 'learned helplessness'—which we'll come back to soon.

Travel Wisely

Simply removing yourself from your immediate situation may be enough to bring some important self-realisations. But travel brings nothing if you simply recreate your usual routine in a difference place. To travel wisely, remove yourself from your usually daily routine and commit *totally* to being in that new space, whether for a few weeks, or even just a few days. You don't need to leave the country—you just need to put yourself in a different place, physically and psychologically. Consider cutting off from social media during this time too. It's a great way of reconnecting with your true self without distraction. You will gain the clarity you need to create a plan that will nurture the real you.

Volunteer

Volunteering allows you to sample different fields of work, make new contacts, gain new skills, and broaden your horizons. It can bring a sense of belonging that may be missing from your work or personal life. It can also help put things in perspective. You may even discover new interests and ideas about the type of work you want to do in the future.

Volunteering doesn't necessarily require a big commitment, though it's better to under-commit than over-commit. It could be as simple as helping an elderly neighbour with their weekly shopping. Or you might decide to commit a certain number of hours each month to a charity or voluntary organisation. You never know where it may take you.

Walk in nature

You only need to take a look at a typical work setting to realise just how starved our senses are on a daily basis. We seem to live in a culture that equates work with suffering, as if it's admirable to be so busy that we deny our own needs.

Things don't have to be this way.

Workplace culture is a transitory illusion. Colleagues or seniors may be as lost as you. None of this matters. Wake up to your surroundings and make the most of them. Take the time to enjoy your environment. If you live in the countryside, this is easily done, but even if you live in the city, it's surprising how much nature can be found close to home. Every place has its own beauty if you're willing to seek it out. Try getting up a little earlier each day—even fifteen minutes can be enough—and take a different route to work. Maybe you can walk to the second of your tube/bus/train stops, or even walk—or cycle—the entire journey. Pay attention to what's going on around you. Take in the sights. Bring your own sense of peace to your daily commute, in whatever form that may take.

Small changes each day will help you open your eyes to the possibility of larger change. They will give you more energy, inspiration, and vision. They will ensure that your decisions and actions are a true reflection of what you do want out of life, rather an escape mechanism for coping with what you don't.

Chapter 2

Understand How You Got Here

'It is no measure of health to be well
adjusted to a profoundly sick society.'

-JIDDU KRISHNAMURTI

In 1941, at Brooklyn College, New York, a young
psychology instructor, struck by the horrors of war,
began to develop a vision of peace and all it entailed
in human nature. He wanted to understand what allowed
human beings to reach their potential, to become their
most fulfilled, lawful, joyful, honest, and individual

selves. He was inspired by a desire to celebrate the human mind at its best, rather than focusing on what could go wrong, as so many had done before him.

He had endured a testing childhood. With few friends for support, he'd had a lonely upbringing, seeking solace in books and the quiet refuge of libraries. As a result, he'd excelled academically and gone on to study law. But he hated it and soon dropped out.

Thank goodness he did.

This studious fellow's name was Abraham Maslow. He ditched law to follow his passion for understanding the human mind, developing along the way perhaps the most famous and influential theory on human motivation. His work is just as relevant to today's modern workplace as it was to life in the 1940s.

Maslow produced a paper that proposed a hierarchy of needs, 'A Theory of Human Motivation'[22] in which he argued that human needs fall into a hierarchy of necessity, with the most fundamental being at the bottom. Once each need is met, the next need within the hierarchy takes priority and dominates behaviour.

Most of us within the developed world achieve the fundamental aspects—our core physiological needs—without barely a thought for them. We have access to air, water, food and, for the most part, we achieve our safety needs; most of us have personal security, housing, and live within a community. However, from this point on, we're not all as equal as you might think.

Next in the hierarchy comes social belonging—our need to love and be loved. Then comes esteem—the need for a sense of acceptance, self-respect, and self-efficacy. Finally comes the need to be able to uphold our values and gain fulfilment from life, to become everything we're capable of becoming. But these needs—belonging, esteem, fulfilment—are often not met, even with all the comfortable trappings with which we're well-accustomed. Why is that?

There are a number of factors at play. We don't necessarily live near our families, and while social media can be a great connecter, it can also be the ultimate isolator; we trade physical proximity for virtual connection. But in the virtual world, things are not always as they seem. We tend to work in large organisations that bring a sense of isolation and insignificance. We may receive insufficient meaningful feedback on our work, and we may not all be proud of what we need to do each day to earn a living. Corporate greed and its downstream organisational pressures don't always allow us to uphold our values. It's no wonder that belonging, esteem, and fulfilment can be pretty tough to achieve.

The US-based polling organisation Gallup has been reporting on employee engagement since the late 1990s, surveying over 25 million employees across 195 countries. And in 2017, only 33 per cent of US respondents felt 'involved in, enthusiastic about, and committed to their work.'[23] A larger global poll [24] found that in the same year, only 15 per cent of workers felt engaged at work, and a further 18 per cent were actively *disengaged*—they actually *hated* what they did each day. The authors defined 'not engaged' as '. . . checked out. They're sleepwalking through their workday, putting time—but not energy or passion—into their work.'[25]

This means that up to 85 per cent of the world's working population may be at best disillusioned sleepwalkers, and at worst actively *hating* the work they do every day. Are that many of us really sleepwalking through our lives?

We spend the majority of our waking hours at work— around 90,000 hours during our lifetimes if working full time. Most of us also have the good fortune to be able to live well, with our basic human needs met for the duration of our lives. So why the disillusionment? How did this happen in a developed society that at first glance appears to offer countless opportunities? Have our life expectations become too high? Or have we been conditioned into ignoring our needs?

Are you working to live, or living to work?

Consider a typical full-time work pattern. A workday may last anywhere from seven to twelve hours, sometimes more depending on the circumstances. There may be additional commuting time. Sometimes, we need to move away from our roots and our loved ones to secure jobs or careers. Many of us also spend the majority of our day sitting at a desk, potentially churning out work with very little creative licence or autonomy. And that's before we even consider the effects of the politics and the personalities.

Modern working routines often involve little to no meaning for us as individuals. Organisations can be immense machines and employees barely-significant moving parts. It can be hard to feel valued or needed. There may be a lack of belonging or rapport. Workplace goals may exist, but it can often be difficult to see how our work has made any meaningful difference. Open plan office spaces, daily working schedules scattered with group brainstorming sessions, an emphasis on collaboration over individual creativity, constant interruption, and little manoeuvre for independent work—all of these contribute in their own destructive ways, especially for introverts. This is not a marriage destined for happy-ever-after. For employee or employer.

Given this obvious disillusionment, and the environmental factors that likely maintain it, the question is this: why is it so hard to break away from the crowd and follow our individual paths?

'There's no point.'

In 1972, American psychologist Martin Seligman came up with the concept of *learned helplessness*. In a series of experiments that may leave dog lovers appalled, Seligman exposed dogs to electric shocks that they couldn't escape or avoid. A separate group could stop the shocks—though not escape altogether—by pressing a lever, which they eventually learned to use. In a later test, when all dogs were provided with an escape route, those dogs previously contained in the environment they couldn't control didn't even try to escape, even though it was perfectly possible. They just lay down and accepted the shocks. Those who'd learned to operate the lever, however, also quickly learned that they could escape . . . and they did.

Sometimes, humans are not so different. When our past experiences become ingrained, when we believe we have no control over our situation, we think we can't change it. We don't believe that success—whatever that might mean to us personally—is dependent upon our own actions. We don't try. We don't even *think* about trying. Without realising it, we become blind to the opportunities for achieving positive change. We simply lie down and accept the shocks.

Learned helplessness may go some way to explaining why we often don't feel able to change things. But what if we don't even realise the problem? What if disillusionment has crept up so gradually that we simply didn't notice?

The 'boiling frog' experiment was conducted by a number of researchers in the 19th century. Allegedly the story goes something like this: the researchers placed a frog in a pan of boiling water, observing it immediately jump straight out again. But when they put a frog in tepid water and gradually heated the water to boiling, the frog didn't escape. It didn't even *try* to escape. It just slowly boiled to death.

Despite the questionable validity of the underlying premise, the story helps us to understand our own responses to increasingly unhealthy work environments. People don't just suddenly wake up one morning, feel discontent in life, and 'jump straight out'. The realisation may be sudden, but the reaction is usually slow. The contributing factors have been brewing for a long time, a slow and often subconscious process with boundaries being stretched ever further, expectations gradually lowering, health diminishing, and personal relationships strained. By the time they become aware of a problem, they may simply be too enmeshed in the system to realise that other options even exist. Or if they do realise, they may have lost the strength of spirit necessary to make a change.

Instead, they internalise the problem and plod on. Those who do express an appropriate and healthy reaction to an abnormal and unhealthy environment may even be made to feel that their own resilience or mental health is to blame. What is a social problem gets medicalised and becomes a vicious circle. They slowly simmer to boiling point, never thinking to jump out of the pan.

What are the wider causes of learned helplessness? Is something so intrinsic to our psyche solely a product of our working environments? Or has something else gone wrong along the way?

Economist and philosopher Barry Schwartz argues that our sense of disillusionment may stem from the incentive-driven culture that's been prevalent since the Industrial Revolution.[26] He suggests that the segregation of labour, designed to lower costs through mass production, has steadily paved the way for decades of soul-destroying and meaningless work. He contends that incentives have been introduced to create an artificial sense of purpose in all this mindless toil.

You may find all this irrelevant—after all, you're not like Charlie Chaplin in *Modern Times*, constantly battling to keep up with the ever-increasing pace of a production line. But if your values are out of sync with your organisation's ethos, it's the same principle. If you're human and you are forced to work towards targets or incentives that are meaningless or valueless to you, you *will* eventually be affected.

But does this all *begin* at work? Or are we already primed for it?

The target trap

A target-driven educational system leaves us with one ultimate message: do the thing that gets results. Targets and results are all that matter.

'When a measure becomes a target, it ceases to be a good measure.' [27]

So noted the economist Charles Goodhart, in an observation that came to be known as 'Goodhart's Law'. In other words, better results are generally a good measure of quality, but as soon as they're relied upon for policy-making purposes, the relationship breaks down.

Yet targets have prevailed. Cheating and gaming the system have become the acceptable norms. In the healthcare sector, targets may come in the form of patient waiting times and survival statistics; in policing, it's crime levels. In education, it's school exam performance—and a 2014 study by the Association of Teachers and Lecturers[28] reported that their members felt under so much pressure to attain targets, that the teaching, learning, and development of their pupils was suffering as a result.

The private sector is similarly packed with targets and bonuses based on performance. They're ingrained, often unpleasant, and usually an unnecessary distraction. The target commands greater value than the work itself.

If we are consistently exposed to an environment in which all that matters is the result, regardless of our enjoyment of the task—or, indeed, the ethics of seeking it—then why do anything of true value at all?

Following our own path and concentrating on something we truly value is often deemed inherently unwise. It's the result that matters, so instead, we learn how to get good results. But how can this end well when we're not learning how to do the things we want to do . . . or even learning how to recognise what it is we want to do? We're learning only what we think we *should* do.

Ironically, the blinkered culture of a targets-driven system makes it more difficult to question the ethics of the system itself. No wonder so many of us reach adulthood in a heightened state of learned helplessness, with relatively little knowledge of our self-worth.

If we become used to adapting ourselves to fit what we believe is expected of us, we eventually lose motivation and inspiration. We can end up in situations and environments that are naturally uncomfortable to us, and because this discomfort is so deep rooted, it becomes familiar.

A self-belief as deeply rooted as this becomes hard to shake off. It has the potential to shape our behaviours and choices well into adult life.

But there is an upside to all this. Our basic needs are already met. We can educate ourselves, learn about ourselves, travel, and choose our own relationships. We can bring more meaning and value to our immediate environment, and we can optimise not just our own wellbeing, but the wellbeing of those around us.

With all of that comes amazing potential.

Chapter 3

Celebrate Introversion in the Workplace

'To be yourself in a world that is constantly trying to make you something else is the greatest accomplishment.'

-RALPH WALDO EMERSON

Workplaces have become increasingly biased towards extroversion. Equality of gender and race has received much attention, but there has been little recognition of different personalities' workplace needs—even though our personality is just as much a part of who we are as our gender or race.

People with introverted personalities tend to recharge by spending time in quieter environments. Being around people, or in high-stimulation situations, for long periods can lead to overstimulation and overwhelm. To function well within the workplace, the following are all important for introverts:

Independence and flexibility

Space and time for concentration

The freedom to be creative

Being able to focus on thoughts and ideas over people and events

The ability to choose one-to-one over group discussion

In recent years, books like Susan Cain's *Quiet* have raised awareness of introversion and its characteristics[29] and there has been a surge of 'best fit' job suggestions published. If you're an introvert, they'll direct you to such professions as writer, archivist, accountant, scientist, and artist. But that doesn't necessarily mean that introverts can't be successful in roles traditionally seen as more outward-facing. Take sales, for example: a large 2001 analysis revealed almost zero correlation between sales performance and extroversion.[30] Why is this?

It may be that this is down to the learned skill of playing up certain behaviours and suppressing one's true nature. But it may also come from listening, reflecting, and generating original ideas, all of which manifest when an introverted person can be themselves and work in a way that suits them. Introverts and extroverts have the potential to perform equally well in high-stimulation situations. It's just that introverts are likely to need more quiet time to prepare beforehand, and more quiet time to recover afterwards.

It matters that introverts work in line with their core values. That's not to say the same doesn't apply to extroverts. But introverts' greater tendency for introspection and self-talk is more likely to lead to disillusionment if this requirement is not met. Values-aligned work can bring great motivation and satisfaction.

The trick is to find the balance between doing something you love and finding a way to sustainably fulfil that role.

If you tend towards introversion, you don't *have* to seek out a traditional introvert-suited job. Aim first for one that is in line with your core values and beliefs, then carve out a way for your personality to thrive within that role. Find a method of working which plays to your unique skills and sets you apart from the pack. Not only will this help you feel more empowered over your life choices; your confidence and self-esteem will soar.

And all of this is becoming easier than ever to achieve. The notion of the workplace is rapidly becoming more fluid and flexible, with remote working well-recognised, and growing recognition of the importance of individualised working patterns and their effect on productivity.

Find a method of working that suits you

Excessive stress has a nasty way of tainting everything else in our lives, making it hard to see objectively what needs to change. It can force us into making drastic and hasty decisions that may not be in our best interests in the long run. If you tackle one issue at a time, you will gain more clarity. You may discover, in the process of implementing these strategies, that the key problem is not your career, but the way you work each day. Through eliminating some of the causes of stress, you may find that what's left is something you actually enjoy and can shape in ways you hadn't previously considered possible.

Let's look at some general strategies that you can try straight away to manage your workplace demands. Try implementing one of them today.

Get downtime

Being an introvert means you may need more time than most to unwind at the end of the working day, especially if that day was spent in a high-stimulus environment. You may struggle if you're required to be in a large group of people continuously for hours at a time, day after day, with insufficient downtime in between. If this is you, try some of these tips to help you cope:

Set aside some time each day to break away, recharge your energy, and process your thoughts quietly. This may mean getting out of the building during your lunchbreak, or scheduling regular five-minute gaps throughout the day to get away from your immediate surroundings.

If your work is largely desk-based, consider organising a proportion of your work week to be spent working from home. If your income allows it, consider working part-time so you can spend the remaining time doing something more creative and meaningful to you.

If you are in a public-facing role, try to spend your breaks away from further stimulation. Avoid noisy canteens or overcrowded staffrooms. Find a place in which you feel peaceful and commit to taking regular breaks there. This is not time wasted—it will increase your energy and productivity during the remainder of the day.

Downtime doesn't have to mean complete silence and isolation either—just try to spend some time each day doing whatever makes you feel most at peace.

Maintain autonomy, independence, and good working relationships

Personality-types aside, evidence suggests employees have become frustrated with the distractions caused by the open-plan office layout[31] and the effect on introverts is inevitable. There is little opportunity for focused, independent working for those who find it harder to filter out external stimuli. The environment is supposed to promote innovation and communication, but it may actually harm employee relations and perceived job performance.[32]

Consider the following to try and improve your independence and autonomy:

Be open and honest about your working style. Ask if there are any small projects which you could take on independently. Perhaps there are areas within the daily workings of the organisation that could do with improvement. This may require time spent away from your usual workplace to conduct research. If so, great— that's more variety, and an opportunity to remove yourself from constant overstimulation. Allow your creativity to come to the forefront. Don't feel that your job description should dictate your job experience.

Ask about extra training opportunities in a different work area. This could be a personal development course, a language class, or training in public speaking. You could become your organisation's first aider and gain basic life support skills in the process. Most organisations will have a training budget and may run internal training on work-related subjects. Provided the training will demonstrably improve the performance of your organisation, either directly or through improved motivation and self-confidence, it's feasible.

Even if it's not possible at work, there are countless opportunities for learning online, as well as through community-based evening or weekend classes. Not only will learning something new bring some autonomy into your life, but you may also discover new skills and interests you never knew you had. And you'll meet like-minded people along the way. Once you open your mind to the prospect of new opportunities in this way, you broaden your outlook and your horizons. Your world will grow and brighten. You will find yourself less reactive to the constraints of micromanagement and inflexibility in the workplace.

If you have any ongoing home-based projects with the potential to bring in income, why not consider starting a business of your own? Perhaps you could negotiate a reduction in your working hours to accommodate increased commitment to your business. This will give you a taste of the self-employed life as well as the freedom of working independently in your own environment. Who knows where it might take you in the future?

Manage conflict

Introverts and extroverts usually manage conflict differently. Introverts prefer to avoid conflict wherever possible—they'll usually try to de-escalate it. Extroverts, on the other hand, are frequently more dominating and assertive—they're less likely to avoid conflict and may adopt a collaborative approach.[33] Unsurprisingly, these approaches are prone to misinterpretation by both parties: introverts may feel that they are being personally attacked, whereas extroverts may feel that the other party isn't as interested in finding a resolution.

When conflict arises—as it inevitably does—bear these points in mind:

Be aware of people who drain your energy. Protecting your emotional wellbeing is just as important as protecting your physical wellbeing. Sometimes invisible harm can be the worst kind . . . and the hardest to undo.

In brainstorming sessions or meetings that involve the generation or sharing of ideas, ensure there is time beforehand for everyone to formulate and write down their own ideas, prior to sharing with the group.

As we've already mentioned, if it's feasible for you, consider negotiating home-working for at least part of the week, if possible. Research suggests that working from home boosts productivity, regardless of personality type.[34] For the introvert, it minimises exposure to conflict, unnecessary stimulation, and energy-draining colleagues. Replacing the daily commute with more rest or exercise may also boost health and general wellbeing.

Avoid burnout

There is evidence that suggests introverts may be more prone to disengagement and burnout at work.[35] Why is this?

It's simple. Introverts prefer quiet surroundings where they can reflect and nurture their creativity. But for many workplaces, the typical environment is full of interruptions, team meetings and brainstorming sessions, an over-emphasis on collaborative working, and large open-plan offices. It's a perfect storm of overstimulation. Introverts simply don't function well under these conditions.

Find your voice in solitude

Introverts can flourish within a team by contributing their ideas. But they'll do even better if they can do at least some of it in solitude. Brainstorming meetings are designed to generate the best possible ideas from a team of people, but by their very nature, they fail to recognise that different personality types generate ideas in different ways. Employees who tend towards extroversion may thrive in group interactions, generating the most ideas out loud. But this doesn't necessarily mean they generate the *best* ideas.

That's not to say that any one personality type is more likely than the other to come up with good ideas. It's just that there's currently a lack of recognition and acceptance that we all have different ways of working and achieving our true potential. After all, a good team works best when its members are given the freedom to contribute their unique skills in their unique way. And for many, introverts especially, this means working alone for some of the time. The ideas of some of the greatest creative minds in history were generated in this way.

But it's not just the generation of ideas that benefits from space and solitude. Introverts are typically deep and imaginative thinkers, preferring to work through thoughts individually before reaching conclusions. This need is often overlooked by the ever-pervasive group decision-making culture. Groupthink is a psychological phenomenon in which individual judgement and perception are lost or distorted due to the desire for conformity or harmony within a group, leading to dysfunctional or irrational decision making . . . often to the detriment of the group as a whole. This loss of individual judgement may not even be a conscious one.[36] So, for introverts, the need for individuality in decision making may be distorted or muffled in the modern workplace.

Challenge learned helplessness

A study at the University of Adelaide put 48 students through two 'training' tasks.[37] They were assigned to either a 'controllable' or 'uncontrollable' group, matched so that levels of introversion were equal across both groups. The students were not aware that they had been segregated, or that an 'uncontrollable' group existed.

They were told that they would repeatedly hear a buzzer. Their task was to try and stop the buzzer, by pressing a combination of switches in a specific order. Once the buzzer stopped, one of two lights would come on: a green light if they had been successful at stopping the buzzer themselves, or a red light if they hadn't and the buzzer had stopped of its own accord. For subjects in the controllable group, there did indeed exist a unique combination of switches that would allow them to successfully stop the buzzer. For those in the uncontrollable group, there was no such combination—they were destined to fail at every attempt, no matter which combination they tried. All students were then tested again—but this time they all had the ability to stop the buzzer.

Interestingly, the introverted students performed much more poorly than the extroverts in the second test, despite no significant differences in performance between personality types per group in the first. It took introverts longer to figure out the correct combination, and significantly more introverts than extroverts failed to work out the combination at all. The introverts essentially showed more learned helplessness following failure in the first exercise.

But why the difference?

It comes down to different learning styles. Extroverts prefer a higher-stimulation learning environment. They prefer group work and can feel drained by working alone. In contrast, introverts tend to learn best in quieter environments. The results are hardly surprising, when you think about it.

Given the right support, we all have the potential to contribute unique interpretations, opinions, and talents to enrich a group. But it doesn't always work out that way. Learned helplessness can result from years of feeling unheard in the classroom. With thirty or more students in a room, there isn't always the flexibility to accommodate everybody, and extroverts may be more demanding of time and attention. Group work and collaboration are seen as key to educational development, with classroom setups that celebrate social learning activities over quiet reflection. And naturally, introverted students are less likely to contribute in an environment like this. They then miss out on the vital confidence building that stems from having their opinions heard, accepted, and used to influence outcomes. And if parents pressurise their children to be more extroverted, it's a double whammy that their natural way of being is not acceptable to society.

There's a real danger of stifling natural talent at an early age.

Avoid pressure to conform

Writing in the Chronicle of Higher Education, US-based English professor William Pannapacker decided to undergo the Myers Briggs personality test, along with his students. He predicted a significant proportion of introverts ('I's) based on prevailing research at the time. But not a single student demonstrated an 'I' type. He wondered why this should be, given that he knew his students well and considered around a third of them to be introverted.

He eventually realised it came down to social stigma. The test included questions with 'socially acceptable' answers such as, 'Would you rather go to a party or stay at home reading a book?' He mused that 'the test may as well have asked, "Would you prefer to be cool, popular and successful or weird, isolated, and a failure?"'[38] The students had simply given the answers they'd thought were wanted, rather than saying how they really felt.

Introverted children may sense that their natural state of being is different from accepted societal behaviour. As a result, they learn to pretend to be something they are not, in order to succeed in the world as they perceive it. This is a learned behaviour that begins in the classroom and persists into adult life, becoming so ingrained that it obscures what we need to thrive. It's little wonder that so many of us neglect our true selves when the time comes to make career choices.

Chapter 4

Get to Grips with Stress

'Problems are not the problem; coping is the problem.'

-VIRGINIA SATIR

Our choices matter. And surprisingly, it may be the small choices that turn out to be the life-changing ones. To make good choices, we need to objectively appraise ourselves and our environments. But we can't do this effectively when we're under stress—in adrenalin-fuelled fight or flight mode we're much more likely to make rash decisions. Stress, and the coping mechanisms that come with it, can rapidly take us off course.

Stress is a major challenge to health and wellbeing and it's on the rise globally. The 2016 'Stress in America' survey revealed that 80 per cent of Americans had experienced at least one symptom of stress in the previous year.[39] It's a similar story in the UK, with stress cited as the top health and safety concern in UK workplaces.[40] In their guidance on mental wellbeing at work, the UK National Institute of Clinical Excellence reported that '530,000 people in Britain believed they were suffering from stress, depression or anxiety due to work at a level that made them ill with an estimated 13.7 million working days lost as a result.'[41]

Sobering statistics? Certainly. Are we doomed to an unhealthy life hampered by stress? Not necessarily.

What is stress?

The stress response is a normal physiological reaction to a perceived threat. It activates our sympathetic nervous system, which triggers a cascade release of hormones, including adrenaline and cortisol, which collectively increase heart rate, raise blood pressure, redirect blood flow away from the peripheries to the essential organs, increase availability of glucose for energy, and suppress other non-essential functions, including the immune and digestive systems. This well-known 'flight or fight' mechanism helps us to survive in life-threatening situations when we need to think and move rapidly—for example when faced with a sabre-toothed tiger. But while we don't often get attacked by extinct predators nowadays, our brains respond in the same way as they did tens of thousands of years ago . . . regardless of whether the 'threat' is real or imagined.

And imagined threats vary from person to person. If you're terrified of public speaking, the prospect of having to give a presentation may cause your body to undergo the same physiological processes as your distant ancestors, when they were confronted by their predatory nemesis. The stress response is a very real and physical phenomenon.

Stress hormones in moderation can be a good thing. They aid performance. The adrenaline-induced racing heart, wide eyes, and quick-thinking brain may just help you get through that dreaded presentation. It's when the stressor become persistent that problems begin, as overexposure to hormones such as cortisol can cause a number of health issues, including raised blood sugar levels, weight gain, increased blood pressure, low mood, and reduced immunity. A study of job-related stress in nurses, published by the Harvard School of Public Health in Boston,[42] found that the health problems associated with it were as bad as those associated with smoking and sedentary lifestyles. Left unchecked, the effects of stress can result in a number of chronic health conditions.

What is it about being unhappy at work that exacerbates stress?

It's all to do with how we react to the tasks put in front of us. Many people mistakenly assume that stress is purely external and that it either exists or it doesn't. Of course, there are general situations which are universally accepted as 'stressful', but a particular stressor can severely affect one person while another may be completely immune to it. This is because the effect of stress is actually based on our *perceptions*. It can be defined as a mismatch between the perceived demands placed upon us and our perception of our abilities to deal with those demands.[43] It's not a gap between *actual* demand and ability—it's the *perceived* gap that causes the stress.

A key factor in this process is our appraisal of the stressful event—what is the stress and what does it mean to us? Is it a threat, a challenge, or insignificant? When stress is viewed as a threat, we see it as something that will cause future harm. But when it is viewed as a challenge, we are more likely to develop a positive response—because we see it as something that could lead to a positive outcome.

We also appraise our coping abilities. These can be categorised as *emotion-focused* (talking about the issues, maintaining supportive friendships, writing, and meditating) and *problem-focused* (learning new skills, developing action plans, seeking information and support). If we feel that we can't deal with the event, stress ensues. As we've already noted, it's not necessarily the event itself which drives the stress, but our *interpretation* of it, its meaning to us, and our ability to manage it.

So, if we don't feel that our job suits our core values, skills, individual needs, and personality, then we are more likely to appraise any associated work demands as exceeding our personal resources. In other words, we're more likely to feel that it is all just too much.

The problem is compounded in introverts. Research has shown that introverts are less likely to appraise stressful events as a challenge,[44] which means they are more likely to view it as causing future harm. In turn, they may feel less able to cope with the same challenge that a more extroverted person may thrive upon.

How does stress affect you?

Stress can affect every aspect of our lives. Sometimes, it's only when we step back and look at the bigger picture that the root cause—the stressor—becomes glaringly obvious.

The effects of stress, known as the 'stress response', may include:

Emotional: You may feel sad, tearful, irritable, and on edge. You may find yourself over-reacting to seemingly minor events, conversations, or situations.

Cognitive: You may find it increasingly difficult to concentrate or make decisions. You may experience problems winding down at the end of the working day or 'switching off'. You may find yourself becoming more self-critical, or more sensitive to criticism from others.

Behavioural: You may adopt unhealthy habits, such as drinking or smoking excessively, in an effort to help regain balance or relaxation. You may experience changes in appetite, leading to eating less or more than usual.

Physiological: In the short term, you may notice your heart beating faster or that you are breathing more quickly. In the long term, you may be at increased risk of physical issues including muscular aches and pains, fatigue, increased susceptibility to infections, and tension-type headaches.

For many people, the effects of stress can continue unrecognised or unaddressed for a lifetime, only later manifesting as psychological or physical illness. That's why being in tune with your body right now is so important. Taking the time to stop, evaluate, and address the issues you're facing is always worth it. The benefits for your future health, peace, happiness, and freedom are beyond price.

The organisational effects of stress

The effects of unhappiness at work don't just stop with ourselves. Individual demotivation and reduced productivity ultimately filter through the whole organisation and impair its overall performance. Personal relationships may become damaged due to stress responses. Low mood in managers can filter down and affect those reporting to them, either directly via their interactions, or indirectly due to the effects on decision making and company culture. Just one powerful person suffering from the negative effects of stress may be all it takes to put a black cloud over the morale of an entire organisation.

Stress depends on our perceptions of the stressor and our ability to cope. But it also depends on our personality. While it has been suggested that extroverted workers are more *prone* to stress than introverted workers,[45] introverts may be less able to cope with it in certain situations, particularly without enough downtime. Extroverts, on the other hand, may be more likely to appraise stressors as challenges rather than threats[46] and show greater perceived coping ability, more control over potentially stressful tasks, and lower *perceived* stress.[47]

This isn't necessarily a bad thing. It means that there is potential for change and growth. We can learn to adapt to stress, regardless of our personality. We can also teach ourselves to adopt healthier coping behaviours. Stress management involves making the emotional and physical changes necessary to control and reduce the tension we experience in our lives.

Minimising stress at work

Minimise interruptions

It's easy to become overwhelmed by interruptions during a workday: email, social media, phone, meetings, systems issues, not to mention the competing demands of colleagues. For introverts, this overstimulation is compounded and leads to exhaustion.

Set aside daily protected time for achieving your job list. Try avoiding emails or messages during specific times each day, using that window to give your full attention to the tasks at hand. If you work in a noisy office, use earphones or earplugs if possible, to filter out background noise. Interruptions are inevitable and often unavoidable, but you can significantly minimise your stress response to them by avoiding an immediate reaction. Calmly accept new tasks if you are able, prioritise, then put them to one side until you are ready to give them your full concentration. You'll be amazed at how much you can get done by adopting this one simple habit. It reduces the immediate physical impact of the stress appraisal process, nipping it in the bud before it has the chance to become overwhelming.

Eat well

You must nurture your health to achieve wellbeing at work. It's easy to succumb to chocolate and crisps in a stressful environment, but instant sugar highs ultimately lead to unhealthy cravings, mood swings, weight gain, and fatigue . . . all of which are likely to reduce your performance and satisfaction at work. Try to eat wholefood-based meals and avoid ultra-processed foods.[48] Eat mindfully. Focus on nutrients rather than calories. Make sure you dedicate undisturbed time for eating, preferably away from your usual work environment.

Write it down

Writing down your thoughts and emotions about stressful events allows you the space to reflect on them objectively. Conversely, when you experience a positive event, write about this too, and how it made you feel. Write about aspects of your day that you are grateful for. Introverts are more likely to derive satisfaction from time and space to reflect in solitude, and writing is ideal for this. It could be as little as a couple of sentences in response to each event—one for the event and one for how it made you feel.

The act of writing slows down your thought processes, reducing the risk of turning reflection into anxiety-provoking rumination. You can vent without causing harm. Writing can give clarity to your emotions and increase self-awareness. By revealing harmful thinking patterns, as well as opportunities and ideas for problem solving, you may discover more about yourself and develop new approaches to old problems. Writing about the positives can help avoid the trap of persistent negative thinking-patterns. It can put reactions into perspective and allow you to realise you may have experienced distorted reactions to certain triggers.

Create a peaceful workspace

Introverts often benefit from a quiet space into which they can retreat after prolonged external stimulation. Clutter in the workspace is distracting and inhibits productivity—and it may add to that chaotic feeling that introverts find so exhausting. Try to leave your workspace clean and tidy at the end of each day. Make the space your own—and as peaceful as possible—with a plant or flowers. This isn't just for aesthetic reasons either; recent research suggests that 'nature' in the workplace may be associated with less perceived stress, as well as improved general health.[49]

Know your limits . . . and stick to them

Saying 'no' can be hard sometimes, particularly when you feel you should be working as part of a team, or if others are depending on you. But accepting more work than you can handle will only increase your risk of burnout. There will always be more work to do. There will always be demands. And if others—managers, clients, co-workers—are not aware of your limits, the demands will continue to pile up.

How you manage this is down to you. It may feel like an achievement to plough through ever-increasing piles of work. You may get some short-term recognition for doing so. However, if you continue like this and say nothing, expectations will continue, and the work volume will simply keep growing.

As an introvert, it takes real courage to speak up and set your limits, but it's worth it. Be clear about your boundaries. Chances are, you'll lead the way for others to speak up too.

We're all human and we all have a breaking point. But why wait to reach that point? Prevention is better than cure.

Build up new support networks . . . and treasure the existing ones

Having a wide support network doesn't have to mean endless networking and socialising. This is a meaningless struggle and an energy-sapping exercise for introverts. Having a support network simply means having a circle of trusted friends, family, and colleagues who know and appreciate you, to whom you can turn for support. They're vital when life gets difficult and you feel up against it.

Try to devote some time each day to connecting with work colleagues who share your values, with whom you feel most comfortable, and with whom you can recharge. This might be just a quiet conversation over coffee or a quick 'check-in' email. Outside of work, consider taking on a new class in any area that interests or relaxes you. You'll meet like-minded people in a low-stress setting, broadening your horizons and opening your mind to new ways of thinking. Close friendships can drift over time, so keep in touch with old friends, even if it's just the odd phone catch-up. Dedicate time to nurturing your personal and family relationships.

The reasons for this are twofold. Firstly, regardless of personality, isolation isn't necessarily about being physically alone—it's about not sharing your reactions, opinions, worries, and plans with those close to you. Isolation can act as a magnifier for stress responses, whereas emotional contact and communication diffuse them. Secondly, a good support network will increase your confidence. It will encourage you to see yourself as valued, supported, and loved. All of this will improve your wellbeing in the long run.

Avoid stimulants

We all know that caffeine can make us more productive at work. However, in the long term, it may exacerbate the effects of stress. Due to its stimulant effects, it can cause problems with sleep, limiting our ability to cope with stress. Furthermore, research has suggested it may increase production of cortisol, adrenaline, and noradrenaline,[50,51] which may in time lead to a number of health issues including raised blood glucose, low mood, impaired immunity, and impaired digestion.

The British Heart Foundation claims that moderate amounts of caffeine should not cause harm for healthy people.[52] But we all have different underlying stress levels. If you're already experiencing workplace stress or stress-related physical symptoms, caffeine (as well as other stimulants) may be best minimised or avoided altogether.

Get enough sleep

We often take sleep for granted and place it low on the list of health maintenance. However, it's probably the most important risk factor when it comes to dealing with stress. Research has demonstrated that insufficient sleep (less than six hours per night) is a significant risk factor for clinical burnout.[53]

Tiredness and fatigue will spill over into every aspect of our lives and are particularly likely to make themselves known at work. Our stress response depends on whether we rate a task as manageable or not—and tiredness increases the risk of perceiving it as unmanageable. Our brains can only cope with so much input without sufficient rest. Rest is, in essence, the recharge mode for our brains. We wouldn't expect our phones to function for long if we didn't recharge them, so make sure you allow yourself time to rest and do whatever you can to get sufficient, good quality sleep each night.

Prioritise

The combination of limited time and a multitude of tasks clamouring for attention takes its toll. Add constant interruptions and its little wonder we experience workplace stress. So, whenever it threatens to overwhelm you, stop. Take a five-minute break. Breathe deeply, get some fresh air, rehydrate. Even a few seconds is better than nothing. Write down everything that needs doing and split them into two groups: urgent and non-urgent. Then rank each group's tasks in order of importance. Starting with the urgent group, methodically work through each task in order.

This may sound painfully obvious—and lists certainly don't suit everyone—but with a demanding workload, it's easy to forget the basics. I couldn't have survived without lists during my hospital rotations. Adequate planning and prioritisation help restore calm and order to chaos as well as breaking up the workload into manageable chunks, reducing that negative appraisal stress response as we begin to make progress. It's a good way to prevent the panicky feeling we get when things start to accumulate. It also serves as an accurate record of the work you're producing, in itself useful for future appraisals and objectively managing others' expectations.

Deal with conflict

A common cause of stress in the workplace is conflict. Conflict between extroverts and introverts is inevitable, due to different ways of approaching the same problem and the misunderstandings of expressions and behaviours. It is all too easy to react, especially if the conflict has triggered a deep-seated emotion.

But pausing briefly can make all the difference. Be aware that we all have different methods of thinking and communicating. Emotional reactions just make things worse, so take a moment to observe others while they're talking. Try to gain a sense of how they might be feeling or thinking. This focuses on them, rather than your reaction, and allows them more time to become aware of their own behaviour.

Conflict also arises when dominant bosses or aggressive co-workers overstep boundaries, though it's not always easy to see it unfolding. It could be anything from aggressive behaviour to unreasonable demands or personal insults. Or it could be more subtle than that. Bullies—for that's what they are—often do what they do simply because they can. They're rarely challenged. They may rise to the top of their respective organisations with ease. They may not realise the damaging effects downstream, on colleagues or their team. Or they may simply not care—between one and four per cent of the population is estimated to have traits characteristic of antisocial personality disorder,[54] which, in essence, involves a lack of empathy. Personality disorders are more common in the workplace than you may think. If you feel you're up against someone who seems to leave a trail of emotional and psychological destruction wherever they go, my best advice is to simply avoid them and limit your interactions to written communication only.

Take an objective view

In any workplace confrontation, try to avoid acting on triggers or impulse. Take a moment to observe your emotions and reflect on them. Do you feel intimidated because your antagonist reminds you of someone from your past? Are you worried that they may be criticising your performance? Do you feel that they are being unreasonable? Taking your emotions out of the equation allows for a more professional response as well as more control over the situation. Knee-jerk reactions rarely lead to helpful responses, for either party. Try to avoid taking things personally.

Develop healthy habits

At the end of a stressful day, it may be tempting to reach for a tub of ice cream or a gin and tonic (or both) to boost our emotional wellbeing, but these responses can easily become habit. They gradually become less effective at helping us to relax and we need more and more of them just to get the same effect. And as we all know, this takes its toll on our long-term health.

There are plenty of health-improving ways to combat stress in quiet environments. These include yoga, gentle exercise, music, fresh air, cooking nourishing food, walking in nature, reading a good book, and simply spending time with supportive friends and family. Any activity that replenishes you and brings you peace is worth making time for on a daily basis. It's getting into the habit that's important. Evidence suggests it may take an average of 66 days to form a new habit.[55] What's more, habits themselves require little self-control, so once healthy habits are formed, healthier stress responses will follow.

Learn how to truly relax

Constant tension can easily become the norm, especially when we spend the majority of our waking hours at work. The more time we spend in a state of tension, the more important it becomes to train the body to relax. True relaxation has countless health benefits, especially when practised daily.

You could try some of these ways to attain a state of deep relaxation:

Meditation
Deep breathing exercises

Mindfulness

Yoga

Massage

Gentle exercise such as swimming or walking

Find one or more activities that work for you and make regular time for them.

Establish boundaries

We all have our breaking points. What's important is that we recognise them and avoid reaching them. You may know that your productivity and energy diminish when you work more than a certain number of hours per day in a noisy environment. Perhaps you need to keep your evenings and weekends completely free from work-related emails and phone calls. Perhaps you need a quiet, undisturbed space for a portion of your working day. You may need to refuse new projects when your days are already full.

We often feel that saying no creates a bad impression and hampers future opportunities, but a healthy level of self-awareness and confidence is an essential time-management and negotiation skill. And sticking to boundaries reduces the risk of overwhelm and burnout in the long run.

Be positive

Introverts are more reflective and less likely to show positivity in their thoughts than extroverts. So, working on positive thinking is a great way for introverts to minimise the effects of stress on the brain.

The first step is to recognise and eliminate negative thinking, which can take on various forms known as 'cognitive distortions'.[56] These include:

All or nothing thinking: Seeing things as either good or bad, with no middle ground.

Mental filter: Dwelling on the negatives and ignoring the positives.

Magnification or minimisation: Blowing negative things out of proportion or minimising positive things.

Overgeneralisation: Viewing a single negative event as part of a continuing pattern of poor performance or defeat.

Personalisation: Automatically blaming yourself for any negative events without considering any other—or even more likely—reasons. For example, your project proposal may have been declined for budgetary reasons, not due to lack of individual merit.

Emotional reasoning: Making assumptions about how things are, based on your feelings. For example, 'I feel like I will never reach my goals, therefore I will never reach them.'

The second step is to practise positive thinking as frequently as possible. The following are useful ways of achieving this:

Identify: Take a look at the negative thought patterns above and see if you recognise any of them cropping up in you from time to time. Is there any specific area of work that triggers these thoughts more frequently? If so, is there anything you can do to minimise them? Sometimes, just recognising the thought enables you to dismiss it before it takes hold. But if the thought perpetuates with a single trigger, it may be a sign that one particular aspect of work is causing you more stress than you'd previously realised.

Evaluate: When you are feeling stressed, take a moment to evaluate your thoughts. If they seem mainly negative, is there any way you could interpret them more positively? Try to make this a daily habit. Eventually, your brain will instinctively focus on the positives first.

Prioritise surroundings: Try to surround yourself with other positive people, both in and out of work. Negative energy can be infectious and counterproductive to achieving real change. Relationships with positive people will in turn affect your mood and provide a healthier means of support should you need to confide or share your thoughts.

Self-care: Try to avoid thoughts that belittle your self-worth or abilities. Don't say anything to yourself that you wouldn't say to someone else. Compliment yourself when you've achieved something you're proud of—your achievements are valid and important. They help cultivate the skills, abilities, and thought processes that allow you to pursue your own goals and be true to yourself. In other words: be kind to yourself.

Be grateful

Set aside a little time each day to acknowledge the things in your life that you're grateful for. All it takes is just a few minutes first thing in the morning or last thing at night. Reflect upon your achievements. Be proud of them. Consider your health and relationships, your home, your support network. Try writing down a few sentences in a daily 'gratitude journal'. There is a growing body of research suggesting there may be numerous positive effects in expressing gratitude, including increased satisfaction with life,[57] improved mood,[58] improved sleep quality and duration,[59] and even reduced mortality.[60]

Take regular breaks

The demands of the modern workplace assume that greater input equals greater output. But there is a limit. Our personal resources are not endless and we cannot be vigilant *all* the time. However, our energy levels, unlike time, are renewable. We are conned into thinking that fewer breaks means more work gets done, but it may well have the opposite effect. Less rest is energy-depleting and generally results in an overall fall in productivity and a corresponding rise in stress levels. In the same way that our brains eventually filter out constant sensations from our conscious awareness, we may lose the ability to pay attention to a task with prolonged exposure to it. In fact, prolonged attention has been shown to *hinder* work performance, through a phenomenon known as 'vigilance decrement'.[61]

Introverts in particular need time to recharge, especially if the working day is long. Try to ensure a short break every four hours, even if it's only for five or ten minutes. You could take a short stroll outside, sit somewhere quiet with a book, or listen to some relaxing music with earphones. Anything that allows you a few moments of peace is what you need. Make it a habit and treat it with the same importance as achieving work-related tasks. There is absolutely no shame in being proactive about preserving health—and absolutely nothing to be admired in overworking to its detriment. Workplace cultures often celebrate the martyr who ploughs on regardless. But this type of culture will only change when people recalibrate their attitudes to what constitutes a productive working life. So stick to your guns and lead by example.

Identify what you can control . . . and leave the rest alone

Stress is infectious. It's easy to absorb and hard to pin down its root cause. The stress appraisal process, as we've seen, is based on our perceptions, which can be distorted by our beliefs and worries.

But the things we worry about are often completely out of our control. For example, you may be worried about the way the economy is going and the knock-on effect it might have on your job security or that much-needed pay rise. You may be worried about an upcoming presentation and whether your audience will warm to you or not, or what might happen in your next annual assessment.

Try to separate what you can change from what you can't. Practice your public speaking for one hour each day in the run-up to that presentation. Make sure your managers are aware of the good work you do and why you are worthy of that pay rise and favourable assessment. Do what you can, a little each day. The rest is simply out of your hands. There will always be promotions that pass you by, tough audiences, market swings, and impossible-to-please bosses. But if you put in the preparation quietly and methodically, a little each day, things will be more likely to go your way. Do what you can, and then stop. Rest assured that quiet, reflective, step-by-step methodical approaches will pay off. Believe it.

A certain amount of stress in life is unavoidable. But it can be manageable, even as an introvert in an extroverted working environment. So, make a commitment right now to spend some time each day developing healthier habits, using the suggestions in this chapter as a springboard. The aim is to teach yourself to respond healthfully to stressors and to gain peace of mind in your daily work.

Only then are you in the best place to make new decisions about your future.

Chapter 5

Recognise the Issues

*'Vision is the art of seeing what is
invisible to others.'*

-JONATHAN SWIFT

L ondon, Canary Wharf, 2001. I was a new intern working in the Corporate Finance division of a well-known investment bank. I had the typical energy of a soon-to-be Economics graduate, bursting to experience financial freedom and the buzz of the city. Everyone wanted this job, and everyone was willing to do anything to hold on to it. Yet somehow I'd got it and I wasn't going to let it go.

The working hours were long, as were the nights out. I can remember going straight from a fourteen-hour day in the office to an evening gathering and somehow ending up on a night-shoot filmset before being invited by a well-known actor to the after-film party at dawn. On more occasions than I dare to admit, we stumbled out of London nightclubs at four in the morning only to be back in the office at nine. I moved in the kinds of circles I would otherwise never have contemplated joining. I rode expensive taxis across the glittering city every night and ate rich, fancy food each day, all paid for by the company. I lost touch with my roots.

And so began a nine-year whirlwind of trading-floor performance meetings, profit and loss statements, daily deadlines, month-end deadlines, year-end deadlines, extravagant parties, and luxury travel—all mixed up with generous pay-rises and bonuses that I hardly expected and could barely keep up with. But I didn't question any of it.

That is until the autumn of 2006. I found myself working on the trading floor in the company's Sydney office. I had only been there a few weeks and I'd just returned from a work trip to Hong Kong. I can't remember what went on that day, but I remember the moment.

It was mid-afternoon and I was at my desk. The office was in one of the huge city-centre skyscrapers with incredible views over Sydney Harbour. I remember looking out at the water in the distance. It should have been breath-taking, but I just took it all for granted. The air conditioning was blasting, the office was teeming with people, everything was alive and bright. I was at the centre of the financial hub. News in the making. Excitement.

And then . . . silence.

I couldn't hear anything. My colleague, who'd been in mid-flow conversation, was looking at me quizzically. His lips were still moving, but I couldn't hear what he was saying. In fact, I couldn't breathe. I politely excused myself and went outside to get some fresh air. As I walked, my thoughts became tumultuous. I found myself questioning everything. What was I doing here? Where were my roots? Did I believe in what I was doing? I realised I had absolutely no idea.

*

For me, recognising the real problem didn't come easily. It took a career change after a decade in the financial sector, a medical degree, four years of hospital medicine, and even more years of travelling and soul-searching—all compounded by the inevitable effects of long-term stress.

A financial career gave me the opportunity to travel the world, have job security, progress, and live comfortably. But despite all this, I simply failed to thrive. Initially, it seemed that the problem was the finance industry and lack of enthusiasm for the work involved. But it went much deeper than that. The real problem was my body and mind reacting to the toxic working environment they were exposed to, day after day, month after month, year after year.

It was the workplace culture that deprived every human of anything resembling personal space or meaningful connection. It was the lack of access to nature and fresh air, the constant bombardment of noise and interruptions. Extroverted colleagues were on a seemingly never-ending energy trip, draining every source of attention they could find. The water was reaching boiling point and I was feeling the pain. Environment matters.

It's hardly surprising that workplaces can affect us so much—we're shaped by our surroundings. We often see the world through the eyes of our colleagues. It's not so easy to step back and see things as they really are. We *do* however have the power and ability to change things, even if we have to swim against the tide. We just need to be clear about our journey's origin—and its destination.

We have already seen that workplace disillusionment may stem from educational demands and early work experiences. Insightful though this is, these are all fixed factors. They have already happened. There is nothing we can do about them now, other than recognise them for what they are, learn from them, and start to see things more clearly.

So what about the modifiable factors? You will likely be exposed to them on a daily basis. Your personality may affect your susceptibility to them. The good news is that these issues are not set in stone. They are not in the past. They are happening to you right now, which means you can do something about them *right now*.

You'll find a job satisfaction questionnaire examining these factors in the Appendix—answer those questions to see how you score. Add up all the statements you answered positively, scoring yourself two points for each one. If your total score is less than 30, ask yourself what's keeping you in this situation. You may be hoping that something will change: maybe you'll get a promotion; maybe your boss will leave; maybe your workload will improve. Maybe getting any of these things will bring transitory relief. But until you change your way of seeing the problems and their solutions, and take action, it's unlikely that anything will improve in the long run.

To make genuine improvements, take some time to examine the root cause of every issue holding you back and take ownership of it. Once you do this, you can take active and effective steps towards real change.

*

> *'No problem can be solved from the same level of consciousness that created it.'*

> *-ALBERT EINSTEIN*

You may think you're managing well with an ever-growing workload. But what if the cause of your unhappiness isn't the workload? What if it's your ability to stand up and say no to unrealistic demands?

Consider a patient with fatigue who visits the doctor. After some tests, the doctor diagnoses anaemia and prescribes iron tablets. Eventually, the patient may start to feel better. Has the patient been cured? No—until the doctor finds the cause of the anaemia, they are fighting a fire of unknown origin. If the patient has an internal bleed, all the iron tablets in the world won't make a scrap of difference to the root cause and very real harm may result. The short-term fix simply masks the underlying problem.

Think about the way you work. Is there anything you find yourself doing more and more just to get by? It could be anything, from an increasing need for caffeine or alcohol, to painkillers, to poor eating habits, to scrimping on sleep. It could be missing your breaks or leaving late every day. It could be developing unhealthy work or personal relationships. Not one of these things is the real problem—they are simply the temporary fixes that mask what's really going wrong.

Clarity matters, especially when times are hard. But true clarity is not easy to achieve. Many people reach crisis point before even beginning to realise something isn't quite right.

What kind of change do you need?

Take some time to reflect on how you got here. Avoid the temptation to brush over the issues. While career change may seem like a great way of starting afresh, unresolved issues have a habit of making themselves known in different guises, regardless of the path you choose.

Try to see the bigger picture. What is the real problem? Maybe you're experiencing a disharmony between your own values and skills and those demanded by your role, your job, or your career. Perhaps you're exposed to excessive stimulation in your daily working environment that you're unable to fully process. Perhaps you have too little scope for meaningful interaction with others. Or perhaps your work problems stem from factors related to your health or personal life. Whatever the issues, try to identify them and relate them to their causes.

Find a quiet space and take a few minutes to do the following. First, identify the issues affecting you at work, and write them down. Secondly, identify each issue as belonging to one of four categories: job, career, health, or personal. Here are some examples to get you going:

Job factors

Micromanagement

Demanding commute

Excessive workload tied to role/job

Boredom

Conflict with colleagues

Low salary/poor salary progression

Personal factors

Lack of a supportive social network

Money worries

Relationship problems

Lack of expectations/awareness of other available options

Addictive behaviours

Health factors

Fatigue/low energy levels

Low mood/anxiety/poor concentration

Insomnia

Musculoskeletal pain

Ongoing chronic health conditions

Insufficient/inadequate workplace adjustments

Career factors

Poor work-life balance/excessive workload tied to career

Lack of enthusiasm for current career

Limited opportunities for progression

Incompatible values with prevailing ethos and culture

Now create a table based on the list you have made. How does it look? Is one column looking a lot fuller than the rest?

Without dedicating time and effort to thinking things through, our thought processes continue to circle in the same unproductive manner and we never get to the heart of the problem. Writing helps to slow down these thoughts and separate emotions from facts. It allows us to narrow our focus and think more clearly, with greater objectivity. Don't try to solve all your problems in your mind—write them down and read them back.

The next step is to prioritise. If health factors are causing most of your current issues, start with that. If it's personal factors, which is the most pressing or severe?

While it's certainly true that some problems are more difficult to solve than others, consider whether there are any steps you could take today to start the ball rolling. You might want to seek advice, counselling, or life coaching if unsure. But don't be afraid to seek help. These are big issues.

If your immediate job or role is the likely culprit, approach your manager with your problems. It's in their interests to keep you engaged and contented in your work. Raising issues and concerns is just as important as carrying out your role and you may find that an open conversation is enough to begin resolving any issues—but if it isn't, be honest with yourself and stick to your limits. It's better to leave a bad situation than stick with it to the detriment of your wellbeing.

Finding a working role and environment that suits your personality is just as important as finding a role to suit your knowledge and experience. When deciding whether or not to take up a job, it's just as valid a consideration as income, pension, travel, and benefits. Yet it often takes a back seat, if considered at all. And it may actually be the most important thing you could consider when choosing a role, job, or career.

Motivation for change

Once you've analysed things objectively, you may realise that a job or role change is all that's needed to solve your issues. Or perhaps you may need to take some time out to address personal or health problems.

If you have analysed the issues and their root causes, yet still feel your job is the culprit, you may want to start considering alternative options, including a different career path.

So, with all this in mind, ask yourself these three fundamental questions:

1. What effect is my job having on my life?
2. What's stopping me from making a change?
3. Are the costs of avoiding change greater than the benefits?

Chapter 6

Be True to Yourself

*'Many men go fishing all of their lives
without knowing that it is not fish they
are after.'*

-*HENRY DAVID THOREAU*

In a wonderful book called *The Misleading Mind*, psychotherapist Karuna Cayton uses the principles of Buddhist psychology to explain that the true source of our dilemmas lies in our own minds. We tend to use labels and to see people in certain ways; we are hurt when others act 'out of character' and we consequently seek to assign blame. Karuna explains that the problem here may not necessarily be others at all, but our own expectations—by relying on our own 'narrative' of others, we fail to see and accept them as they really are. Thus, by extension, we also fail to acknowledge that we are all in a state of constant change.[62] Essentially, we are setting ourselves up for disappointment.

Could this same 'narrative' concept apply to ourselves? A double life consisting of the factual, in the moment, day to day reality of what happens to us versus the personal narrative we create through our *memories* of what happens to us?

We label ourselves. Like any story, our personal narrative may well be captivating. But it isn't necessarily representative of our true selves. It's often merely a representation of how we feel we *should* be, or how we think others would like to see us.

The career ladder concept facilitates an incredibly motivating narrative—even when it's the wrong ladder. What's more, who says it even needs to be a ladder? Why not a windy path leading to a beautiful destination with some scenic distractions along the way? Regardless of how we choose to view the journey, it's important that the choice of destination is our own, not one chosen because it fits well into others' narrative. The further down the latter path you venture, the harder it becomes to see what is fact and what is fiction or narrative. It becomes harder to extricate yourself.

Think about your own path. Have you ever made a decision based on what others may have thought? Have you ever chased something based on outward image alone? Or gone against what your gut told you was right because it didn't fit with the 'you' you wanted—or needed—to portray to the world?

When we become swept up in our own narrative, we act—or fail to act—out of fear. We don't put our true identity first. We live a life of pretence. Sooner or later, something's going to buckle under the strain.

Keep it simple

Just because you're thinking of changing direction doesn't mean you need to map out the rest of your life.

You don't need to find some elusive passion that will set you forever on the right track. There's no such thing as a 'right track'. There's only the path you carve out for yourself. There's no right or wrong time to make that change; there's only the right time *for you*. You can (and probably will) change track again in the future, because things change as we grow and expose ourselves to new experiences and new people.

The world of work is changing too. A job is no longer necessarily for life. This means you don't need to be able to predict your future. You do, however, need to know your core values and unique skills. Any role, in any profession, that nurtures these things will give you meaning and fulfilment. Productivity and success will follow.

Cast the net wide

By becoming too focused on specifics in the early stages of considering change, you may end up missing opportunities that suit you much better. You could even end up right back where you started: same frustrations, different profession. Job or career titles can be misleading and they're rarely what we perceive them to be. It's tempting to set off at high speed down a new path before fully visualising exactly what's at the end of it, how we'll get there . . . and how we might feel once we do.

At the start, you are simply searching for a unique way of being that suits you. This, in essence, is unlikely to change. Knowing this and staying true to it will allow you to keep steering your course in a way that continually fulfils you throughout your life.

So, take some time now to explore who you are and what it is you want. Think in terms of a role's core principles or the working methods that it entails. Know your values and stick to them. Don't get distracted by cultural impressions and don't fall into the trap of wanting to do what you think you *should* want to do; don't relentlessly pursue a specific job title without considering the implications. Separate yourself from the pull of the rat race and try not to compare yourself to others.

Rather than visualising a title or label and pursuing it at all costs, reflect once again on who you are and what you need from your work. Think about the causes you support the most and the industries that are most in line with your own values. Think about how you could add most value by working in the way you feel most comfortable. Consider the type of immediate working environment you require to be productive. And be clear on the types of environment or working conditions that you're not willing to tolerate.

Sorting through this first is important. These are the aspects of life that will make or break your ability to keep going, regardless of the specific industry or role. They will eventually impact on your wellbeing one way or another. By taking the time now to address all of these things, you are effectively preparing to navigate any obstacles that may appear along the way.

So, what does your ideal work environment look like?

Perhaps you crave the independence and freedom of self-employment. Or maybe you want the variety of two different part-time roles. Perhaps you hope to spend most of your time working outdoors, or to have a job with lifelong scope for continued learning and research. Maybe you want your job to be location-independent, allowing you the freedom to travel and settle anywhere in the world that suits you. There are as many possibilities as there are people.

When you find an appealing job or career prospect, ask yourself what it is about the role that you find most attractive. For example, it could be the scope for flexible working, or the opportunity to help the public. Whatever it is, will it meet your expectations in the current climate? Could you achieve it in your current role, with some changes? Is there any other job that would allow you to achieve it, while also offering a more nourishing way of life that suits your personality?

For now, just be clear about the general methods of working that enable you to thrive. Passion and productivity will follow if it's the right fit for you.

'What do you want to be when you grow up?'

When we're children, everything seems possible. Fear of judgement doesn't even enter the equation when we dream of 'what we want to be'. But when we finally reach the real world of work, we're asked 'what we do for a living'. Notice the change in language—*be* becomes *do*. Our dreams and plans are built around 'being'; we look to 'becoming' something, rather than simply 'doing' a job. We change our personal narrative—how we see ourselves and how we imagine others see us. Our identity may become so tied up with what we do that we become afraid of challenging it.

The problem is this: all the focus is on an imagined identity at the expense of how we function best and how we already live our day-to-day lives.

Consider again your reasons for choosing your current job and the expectations that drove this choice. Nowadays, the lines between different professions are more blurred than ever. Jobs and workplaces are becoming increasingly compartmentalised and standardised. True creative and independent work is becoming harder to achieve within the confines of an organisation. Even the caring professions are crammed with administrative demands, leaving little room for spontaneity, creativity, or autonomy. Over-reliance on controls can rob highly-skilled professionals of the ability or desire to think like human beings. Be sure to think about the true nature of a job and all it entails *in the present day*, not just in its traditional cultural impressions. Take any opportunity you can to gain experience in that field to ensure that you're basing your decisions on the best type of information: your own experience.

When I first considered a career change out of the financial sector and into healthcare, I was interested in complementary therapies and nutrition. I loved the idea that many of the answers we seek—at least when it comes to healthcare—are already provided for us in nature. I didn't see these as replacements for traditional medicine, but as additions to it.

As I began to share my dreams, I wasn't always met with encouragement. Back then, the concept of integrative medicine wasn't the hot topic it has since become. What people thought mattered to me. But in the whirlwind that ensued, I completely forgot all that had inspired me in the first place. I became focused on one milestone after another, all with the end goal in mind:

finish a well-recognised course, get the qualification, live up to expectations. That was all that seemed to matter.

And then, one day, with all those achievements safely in the bag, I found myself burned out, heavily fatigued, and beginning to question it all. The influencers whose opinions had once mattered so much were no longer in my life. My once strong and steady support network had dwindled in the race to achieve. This time though, I wasn't in the comforts of a quiet and luxurious office in the finance industry—I was in the depths of an aged, crumbling hospital ward, buried in struggling NHS systems, harsh conditions, and a firefighting approach to medicine that seemingly had nothing to do with attaining health. It was a world away from the type of healthcare that I had originally wanted to practise. How had I ended up in this position again? How could I have come so far off track?

I had simply got lost in the wrong narrative.

Remembering what drove me to healthcare in the first place, I began to rediscover my interest in nutrition and complementary therapies. But I struggled to reconcile this with the surgical culture I had found myself in. Eventually, I realised I still had a choice, if I was willing to change my thinking. I didn't have to do what every colleague was doing. I didn't have to enter yet another rat race. I realised that 'healthcare' involved so much more than modern medicine as we know it. The healthcare landscape was evolving rapidly.

So, I devoted my energy to developing skills that could help people in other ways. I studied medical acupuncture and furthered my knowledge of nutrition with a master's degree. I became interested in medical writing and the power of inspirational education materials for improving food choices. I ran health coaching clinics. These activities were in line with my core values. They didn't feel like work. In dedicating my time and energy to them, I gained extra energy in return. It was a two-way street. And, most importantly, they allowed me time and space for quiet reflection and creative thought, the ability to learn and grow independently, and the chance to help others in a meaningful way.

The same principles apply in any role, job, or career. There are many different paths you can take in expressing what they mean to you, if you are willing to think differently. Just because a certain route is seen as the most sought after, that doesn't mean it's the best path for you. The best path for you is the one that allows you to be yourself. The more you think—and believe—this, the more you will make decisions that reflect it. Not only will you thrive, but you will also likely reap the rewards of setting yourself apart from the competition as someone truly passionate about, and dedicated to, their field.

As you start on your path, I encourage you to think deeply about what makes you tick. Is your personal narrative true to who you are? What do you need to be able to thrive, not just to survive? If work is taking its toll, don't be afraid to see it for what it is and speak up for what you need. Don't be afraid to walk away from a situation that robs you of your peace. Any trade-off that impacts your health and wellbeing simply isn't worth it.

Consider where you want to be. Put yourself first. In the end, this will create a sense of peace and fulfilment that can only benefit those around you. You will go on to reap the rewards for sure.

Chapter 7

Find Your Vocation

*'Find your bliss and the universe will
open doors where there are only
walls.'*

-JOSEPH CAMPBELL

During my first few hospital rotations, I began to witness just how swiftly and totally a toxic work environment could decimate wellbeing. And it took time to realise that this had nothing to do with the essence of being in a caring vocation. It was the system. The hierarchies and bureaucracy. The underfunding and lack of autonomy.

But for me, most toxic of all was the constant stimulation. You're no use to anyone if you're overloaded. Quiet surroundings conducive to productivity and creativity helped me to function. I began to suspect that this might be the case for some of my colleagues too. But to embrace this need meant overcoming the prevailing cultural belief that 'quiet time' equated to being workshy or not committed fully to the cause—which couldn't have been further from the truth. I eventually recognised the need to stay true to my needs and values. In the end, it paid off. I was able to do more meaningful and sustainable work, in a state of good health, while achieving all the successes I had wished for.

What is a vocation?

What does 'vocation' mean? Can we all have one? And how is it different from a job or career?

We tend to use those last two words interchangeably, reserving 'vocation' for a select few professions. But vocation isn't necessarily all about a profession. It is simply a way of being your true self.

Let's start by setting straight what these words mean. A job is any situation involving payment in exchange for labour. A career refers to a series of jobs in the same field and implies a certain level of expertise and progression. The word 'vocation' comes from the Latin verb *vocare*, meaning 'to call' and is why a vocation is often referred to as a 'calling'.

A vocation involves doing work that is most in line with who we truly are. We can derive deep fulfilment, satisfaction, and happiness from a vocation. Consider three people who all have the same job. The nature of the job depends on what it means to them. The first sees it as a good way of earning money and allowing them to spend time with their family. They don't care about the job—it is solely a means to an end. The second person sees the job as a step on the ladder towards their goal of being a manager. They want promotion, money and a title, and this job is a stepping stone. The third takes pride in doing the job because they know they are adding value to the people they serve. They have flexible working conditions, are earning enough to survive, and are content with this. They are happy where they are.

None of these people necessarily have it better than the rest. It's all about finding the best fit. A vocation doesn't necessarily have to be the work you do to earn a living: an accountant may have a vocation as an artist; a nurse may have a vocation as an entrepreneur. The question you need to consider is this: do you want to do the thing you love to earn a living, or do you want to earn a living to do the thing you love?

Break it down

Make a list of a typical workday's usual tasks. Then make a second list, comprised of *aspects* of your work. These can be positive or negative aspects—just write down all the things that come into your mind. For example, 'lots of meetings', 'pleasant colleagues', or 'long commute'. Finally, review both lists and colour each item according to the following scheme:

Blue: You thrive on these tasks or aspects of your work. You feel that they make good use of your skills, bring meaning to your work, and allow you to thrive in your working environment.

Green: You put up with these tasks or aspects of your work because you know they have to be done or because you are told to do them. You neither enjoy nor hate performing them, but they add no value to your day and bring you little fulfilment or sense of purpose. You put up with them, but you wouldn't actively choose them.

Red: You dread having to do these tasks. You put them off or avoid them as much as possible. You hate this aspect of your work and find it soul-destroying. Just the thought of these things tends to bring a sense of anxiety and unease. They may cause anxiety even when you're *not* at work.

For all those items highlighted in red, ask yourself the following three questions:

1. What is it about this task/aspect of work that makes me feel like this?

2. What is it about *me* that makes me feel this way?

3. If I could change this task/aspect of work to make it ideal for me, how would I do so?

What do you really need?

Knowing your needs and sticking to them allows you not only to find a role you do best, but one that does best by you. Just as the best type of medicine is holistic—it treats the whole person and not just the disease—the best role for you fulfils all your working needs, not just the need to get paid.

Now, give yourself an hour of undisturbed time to go through the following exercise. Go somewhere comfortable and neutral; searching questions are best approached with peace and clarity, away from triggers and influences.

Values

Values are a part of who we are. They shape how we think and behave in each moment of our lives. They are different to goals in that they can't be achieved or worked towards. They just *are*. They influence what drives us. We experience authentic fulfilment when we're able to uphold our values—and we experience disillusionment when we can't. You may find it hard to live authentically if you spend all your time working in an environment that contradicts your core values. Don't be fooled by labels or 'should be' thoughts; if your gut tells you something is out of sync, it probably is. Trust your feelings.

What moves you?

What makes you most angry, or happy?

Don't analyse too much, just observe the first few things that come to your mind. It could be health, wealth, security, fairness, stability—anything. Try to come up with at least five.

Skills

What unique skills can you offer right now?

What do you do best and how could you relate this to a future role?

What are your unique strengths and what sets you apart from those around you? Strengths don't have to be work-related. For example, they may be as a result of difficult life experiences away from your work. Consider everything that has made you the person you are today.

Use of skills

Do you want to use your skills to teach others? In which case, do you prefer this to be in a one-to-one or in a group setting? Or are you better at communicating through writing?

Do you want to use your skills to help others?

Do you want to be able to build or create something?

Do you want to solve complex analytical problems?

Do you want to contribute to research?

Think about your own life experiences and what has shaped you the most. How could you use those experiences to contribute to the world in a meaningful way? Is there an unmet demand you can visualise? Don't allow yourself to be confined to jobs or careers you already know of; focus on the world as you see it and where you feel your skills could be put to best use.

Interests

What subjects or aspects of life truly capture your interest?

What do you like to read about most in the news or in general?

Is there something you've always wanted to know more about, something that brings out a thirst for more knowledge?

Think openly and broadly. Don't just think in terms of education and don't follow a structured process for reviewing a list of previously held interests. Think about what you would love to learn more about.

Working environment

Do you want to work for an employer that gives you clear, structured expectations, or do you prefer to work independently and carve out your own path?

What type of working environment allows you to thrive?

Where have you produced your best work in the past?

Where do you go when you need to get work done?

The role that's right for you will meet all of these needs to a certain extent. Any trade-off will depend on their relative importance for you individually. Most importantly, remember that any job, career, or vocation that consistently fails to meet any of your needs at all, will eventually cause you problems.

Don't underestimate the power of completing this thought-provoking exercise. The more you are aware of what you need from a role, the more likely you are to recognise an opportunity worth nurturing—and one that will nurture you in return.

Chapter 8

Beat the Barriers

'Fears are educated into us, and can,
if we wish, be educated out.'

-*KARL AUGUSTUS MENNINGER*

B y now, you're getting to know yourself better, discovering new strengths, and stepping outside your comfort zone. You've also created a clearer picture of the working life you need. But is that enough to guarantee that these things will come your way?

Not necessarily.

The truth is you need to *make* these things happen. To make things happen, you need to get the wheels moving. You can't steer a vehicle in any direction until you're in motion. You need to ask yourself some important questions, set some goals, and put some expiry dates on them. Arduous as this may sound, it's the only way to make your dreams happen.

This chapter will take you through some exercises to bring you greater clarity on why you want change, on the obstacles that may be holding you back, and on how to overcome them.

Motivating factors for change

Revisit the job satisfaction questionnaire discussed in Chapter 5. If you're still scoring less than 30 and you want things to improve, it's time to instigate a change.

We've looked at general factors driving disillusionment at work. Now, we'll consider what's driving you personally. Make a list of your own top five motivating factors for change. Here are some common examples to get you started.

More to offer

Many people who feel stuck in their careers experience the constant niggling sensation that they simply have more to offer. The job isn't getting the best out of them and they are unable to be their true selves at work. This leads to the repeated sensation that their days have been wasted.

Unfulfillment

It could be that work is generally not fulfilling for you. Perhaps the company ethos isn't in line with your values, or perhaps the type of work you're doing isn't challenging you enough. It may that you don't have the opportunity to stand out as an individual. Or it may be that you lack any form of control over your working patterns or conditions.

Could do better

You may be thinking that you could get a better job, but you don't know how or where to achieve it. Perhaps you feel constrained by the expectations of, or loyalties to, those around you.

Feel undervalued

As much as we'd all like to wish otherwise, for most of us this is a big factor in the long run. If you feel consistently underpaid and undervalued, this will doubtless be a motivating factor for seeking change.

Boredom

Perhaps you're simply bored with your current working conditions. Maybe you need a new project. Perhaps you crave a more demanding role. Although stability is important for health and wellbeing, we all need differing amounts of variety in our lives. Boredom can lead to low mood and loss of engagement at work. Many organisations are so large that unless you are one of the

135

small minority in a senior position, it's easy to feel more like a statistic than a human being.

Barriers to change

What is it that distinguishes the person who instigates change from the person who stays where they are? Often, it's because the roadblocks seem impassable to the latter. Consider carefully what might be holding you back, and what you might do to mitigate each factor. Below are the most common barriers to career change, with some tips on how to overcome them.

Money

Some career changers may be fortunate enough to see an immediate gain in income. But if you're considering a complete career change, or going self-employed, chances are you'll endure a short-term loss as a trade-off for greater long-term contentment . . . and eventually, greater long-term income. There are so many temptations to spend money in the modern, social media-driven world and it's easy to develop the habit of living within our means; we spend what we have because we can. But we don't necessarily have to. Take a good look at your current spending habits and try to get rid of the non-essentials. Then consider whether you could make any further changes to reduce the cost of your essentials. Estimate what you realistically could get by on each month if you made the changes. Develop a plan to build up a safety net of savings, so that you have a buffer if or when you need it.

You may eventually need less than you originally thought to get by. Even if your estimate is higher than you think you can achieve during your transition, there are always other ways of reducing the essentials. Relocation may be an option to reduce the cost of living. You may even discover newfound sources of health and wellbeing by living outside of more expensive central locations.

Failure

Life changes are daunting. The more time you've spent on your current path, the more invested you are in sticking to it. Leaving that path entails risk: setting up a small business doesn't guarantee an income; going back to college doesn't guarantee a new job at the end of it. You could even make a career or job change and realise you're not suited to it after all.

Our definition of failure has a lot to do with our personal narratives. Try not to exaggerate setbacks or allocate too much meaning to them. They do not reflect on who you are. Every success story involves setbacks; it's how you react to them that matters. Try to see setbacks as opportunities for learning and gaining new transferable skills on your journey to success. Make sure your goals reflect your true self and your true needs. Goals can incorporate the skills you're gaining along the way and they can be revised as you learn from your setbacks. Remember that no experience, good or bad, is ever wasted if you learn from it. The journey can be just as much fun as the destination. Positive thought is a powerful tool indeed.

My career change journey took me down many new avenues. Along the way, I met some inspiring people, made new friendships, and went to places I would otherwise never have visited. I learned about life and its fragility, how to live peacefully on very little money, how to face setbacks, disappointments, fears, and how to be physically and emotionally independent. I learned my limits and the importance of sticking to them. Regardless of the long-term outcome, I could never regret having tried, because I knew that my goal went deeper than just gaining a new title or even a new career. For me, it was about finding a more meaningful way of living.

So, if fear of failure is holding you back, try to focus on what you want to gain from your career change. Remind yourself of your values and interests. Tell yourself that along the way you will focus only on the positives and treat the challenges as opportunities for learning and growth. Don't tie your goal to something that doesn't hold true meaning for you or shape it around a label. Don't worry about what will please others, or what they'll think of you. Know that you will become wiser and more whole just through the process of change. You will feel lighter, freer, and more in line with your true self, right from the start of your journey.

Identity loss

Your current career may be the only one you've ever known. You may see the resultant skills and knowledge as too specific to transfer elsewhere. Understandably, the thought of losing your work identity may leave you uneasy.

Try to remember that you have much more to offer the world than just the skills linked to your current role. Think back to what you used to enjoy. Reconnect with old friends. Be open about the things that matter to you. Often, just saying these things out loud makes them more real and they take on a whole new importance. Consider spending more time with those closest to you. Go on daytrips, go for walks, take up new hobbies. Take on some voluntary work in an area that interests you. Remind yourself that there is much more on offer to you than the job you do right now.

Limiting thinking patterns and behaviours

Our upbringing, education, culture, and environment all contribute to the way we see ourselves. But it may be that making major life changes isn't in your nature; you may have always done what others say is best for you and simply worked from one target to the next.

Try to identify repeating patterns in your working life. For example, you may be overloaded with mundane responsibilities or surrounded by energy-draining colleagues and toxic working environments. Have you become so familiar with these situations that, subconsciously, you've 'settled' for them?

Examine your own beliefs about work. Do you believe that this is all there is? Are you able to stick up for yourself and set clear work boundaries? Observe how you are contributing to how your life is panning out. If you can identify how your thoughts and behaviours are maintaining the status quo, you can start to change them. For example, next time you're faced with a new task that you don't have time for, say so. When you're surrounded by colleagues in conflict, play no part in the dispute and remove yourself from the situation. Get into the habit of visualising the work life you want every day. Soon enough, you'll train your brain into a newer, healthier way of thinking. Your life decisions and subconscious behaviours will favour your goals.

Uncertainty

Change and uncertainty go hand in hand. You may have become familiar with your work role and its routine. Even if you've decided on change, it may be difficult to visualise exactly what you want to do, or how to do it. You may be worried about the uncertainty of finding a job in your new career, or that it won't work out.

Big change doesn't usually happen overnight. Career change is a slow process comprised of small steps. There will be uncertainties along the way, but you will remain in control of them. You can mitigate most of them. You just need to make a start.

Prestige, respect, and trust

You may have grown used to the benefits associated with a particular role. Changing direction may bring a fear of losing others' respect and/or understanding.

Examine more deeply how you actually see yourself, rather than how you think others may see you. Changing direction doesn't necessarily mean letting go of all your experience and training—it means following a path better suited to you at this point. Clinging to a role for perceived status alone will only lead to more disillusionment in the long run.

Obstacles

Career change is not easy. There are likely to be trade-offs along the way, like relocation or a return to education. You may need to take on a period of voluntary or lower-paid work to build up new skills. A new start from a lower rung of the so-called ladder may mean difficulty in relating to your new peers. There are likely to be many obstacles at every stage along the journey of change. But with every hurdle you overcome, your confidence will increase.

Remember that obstacles come up in life regardless. It's the unexpected obstacles we fear the most. There's no point in dedicating energy to worrying about things you cannot predict or control. You can, however, predict and control *some* of the obstacles you're likely to face, and prepare yourself for them.

Discouragers/being judged by others

There will always be naysayers. Making dramatic changes takes courage, so hold firm. All that matters is the judgement and encouragement you give yourself.

Seek objectivity from others when they give you their opinions. Their discouragement may come from a place of either fear or envy. Seeing a colleague breaking away can cause unease, as it forces people to look more closely at themselves and question their own choices. This can be a difficult, painful process. It's easier to deny such feelings than to face them and act upon them. Beware the opinions of those who are invested in you staying put. The people that matter most in your life will understand that your health and happiness come first, and they will want to support you.

Destructive thought patterns

Vertical success is all that matters

There are many forms of success besides money and promotion. What does money matter if you spend so much time working that you don't have time for your family and friends? Think about the type of life you would like to lead and shape your work goals around that.

There's only one route to success

It's no longer true that what you want in life will come to you if you wait long enough. You could stay in the same place your entire career, holding out for promotion and success, and still be made redundant before you get there. The world of work is rapidly changing, and a wide range of skills and life experiences are becoming increasingly valued. Opportunities are gained by new thinking, and by daring to dream.

I should only have one career

Improved communication, travel, and access to information online have opened up a world of opportunity for those who wish to expand their skills. There is no such thing as 'should' anymore. You can contribute great things in a career during the time it brings out the best in you, but you don't have to do this for the rest of your working life. If a job starts to impact your health, wellbeing, and peace of mind, you must consider whether moving on is less harmful than staying put. Sometimes a change of job is sufficient to put things right; sometimes a full career change is needed. The point is that there's an amazing world of opportunity out there for those not tied down by 'should'.

I want to be a specialist at something

Our working lives span 36 years on average.[63] It's not true that you can't master a new skill, at any age. If you are focused on achieving your goals, and you are prepared to put in the time and effort, you can become a master of anything you set your mind to.

My family / children / friends need me

Think carefully about what your family need of you. We all need an income to survive, but those who love you will want you healthy and happy first. Many people spend their entire lives in jobs they hate, purely for financial gain, forgetting that the provision of time and emotional/psychological support is just as important. Think about how your family sees you. If you have children, they need a role model as much as they need financial support. Striving for change, upholding your values, and seeking work that's meaningful to you, will teach them to develop similar core values. Your health, happiness, and the creation of memories is the greatest gift you can give those who love you.

Better to be safe than sorry / it's too risky to leave

It's true that timing is important. But if 'better safe than sorry' is always the first thought in your mind, nothing will change. The risks of change are mitigated by taking small steps. You can taste new experiences, gain new skills, and research new options without leaving the security of where you are now. Just by taking these small steps, you'll gain momentum and eventually start to meet others on the same journey. As you build up new contacts, you'll become more aware of new opportunities and the right ones for you will present themselves. It's down to you to take advantage of them. You'll regret not trying them more than you'll regret staying put—but there's no shame in returning to your previous role in the long run either.

No one is ever truly ready for change—it happens bit by bit, as a result of bringing a visualisation to reality and it starts with the realisation that staying still is no longer an option. At that point, it's time to start clarifying what you want and making it happen. And it surely will . . . if you're willing to make the journey.

Chapter 9

Discover the Power of Goals

*'A dream is just a dream. A goal is a
dream with a plan and a deadline.'*

-HARVEY MACKAY

What are goals . . . and why do they matter?
A goal is a specific outcome we desire to
realise our ambitions. It can be short-term
or long-term. Goals are essential to meaningful change;
they give us purpose and direction. Without clear-cut
goals, drift occurs. There are plenty of distractions in life

to keep us more than occupied, so you need a means of actively diverting your attention towards getting to where you want to be.

The subconscious mind is powerful. When a goal has positive connotations, our subconscious begins to work towards attaining it and we gain energy and drive. Suppose your long-term goal is to write a book. The repeated visualisations of the endpoint—of having a completed book in your hands—bring about positive feelings associated with that desire, acting as a powerful driver to planning, and taking, the necessary actions. Creating vivid images of goals as if they were already achieved and imagining the enjoyment acts as a mini-reward to the subconscious mind, which becomes more responsive; it becomes attracted and attractive to people, resources, ideas, and knowledge that will help you achieve your goals.

Ultimately, having goals helps us in four key ways:

1. They direct our attention towards activities that help achieve the end result, and away from irrelevant activities.

Rebecca Healey

2. They act as a driver for increased effort and energy.
3. They encourage greater persistence.
4. They provide a means for drawing on our current knowledge and expertise, or for attaining new knowledge and expertise.

Goal setting—maximise your chances of achievement

Effective goals need to be **S.M.A.R.T.**, regardless of where it is you wish to get to. The SMART mnemonic is broken down into the following sections. By putting in a little effort to get things right at this stage, you will reap the rewards later on.

S—Specific

Your goals should be clear and unambiguous. Specific terminology paves the way for formulating a plan. What is it you want to accomplish? If your goal is simply to be happy, that's great—but it means nothing unless you examine what happiness actually means to you. Does it mean a better work-life balance? If so, how many hours per week do you want to work? Maybe happiness is being able to work in solitude, or with a particular group of people. Perhaps you want to work from home, or outside in nature.

The more specific you can be, the better you will be able to visualise your goals and turn them into a realistic plan. Specificity gives clarity, allowing you to focus on the goal.

M—Measurable

How will you know when you have achieved your goal? What is your measure of success? Is it earnings-related? The achievement of a professional title or qualification? The ability to change someone's life for the better? Whatever it is, try to make it quantifiable and measurable.

A—Action-oriented

To achieve a goal, you have to do something to get there. There will be steps that you need to take. Actively taking them will give you control over the end result. Opportunities may not exactly fall into your lap, but you can take action to bring them about.

R—Realistic/Relevant

Your goals need to be attainable. A goal with an unrealistic timeframe or unattainable short-term gain is a set-up for failure. Be prepared to review and adjust timescales or the level of gain to set yourself up for success. Set reasonable short-term targets that align with your long-term goal. The more you break down the end result into manageable chunks, the easier it will be to attain. Any long-term goal is daunting without a series of achievable steps along the way. Taking that first step is much easier when it's a small one.

The goals you set should also be relevant. They need to be in alignment with your long-term aims. For example, if you want to achieve a new qualification, it will involve a number of short-term goals such as completing assignments and routine assessments. A long-term goal of becoming self-employed will require short-term goals that focus on gaining the tools required to set up, maintain, and eventually grow your new business.

T—Timebound

Goals require an end date so that they can be properly measured. You won't know how far you're progressing unless you have a point of reference in time. If your goal is to save money, specify the time period. Setting a deadline for reaching your goals increases the likelihood that you will achieve them.

Set aside some time now to write down your most important goals, both short-term and long-term. As an example, let's suppose an employee with a marketing background decides to set up a small business offering online marketing services to help local tradespeople gain more clients.

A good short-term SMART goal could be: *I will acquire skills in budgeting, accounting, and business strategy, through studying and attending an evening or online class. I will aim to achieve certification for my skills within one year.*

A poor short-term goal would be: *I want to know how to run a business.*

A good long-term SMART goal might then be: *I will be in a position to leave my full-time job and be fully self-employed through my business within four years. My job will not be location or time specific, allowing me to work more flexibly from anywhere in the world.*

A poor long-term goal would be: *I want to be able to leave my company and go self-employed, as I want a better work-life balance.*

As you can see, 'One day I would love to . . .' sounds great, but lacks substance. The above example highlights the difference between someone who achieves their goals and someone who doesn't. SMART goals pave the way for taking specific action and eventually achieving the desired change.

Paving the way for success

Write it down

Get your goals down on paper and regularly re-read what you've written. A new design begins with a blueprint. Writing solidifies the goals and forces you to think about the detail. Goals that exist only in your mind have less substance. Your subconscious aligns with your goals once you have them laid out in front of you. Writing them down creates accountability, starts to bring the dream to reality, and gets you into a mindset of achievement.

Visualise

Visualisation means using our imagination to create a mental image of something we want to happen, but that hasn't happened yet. It allows us a glimpse of our desired future. We're able to 'see' the possibility of reaching a goal through actively imagining ourselves doing it, creating a sense of familiarity which, in turn, prepares and motivates us to achieve it.

Research using functional MRI has reported that the brain may interpret imagined events in a similar manner to real events;[64] our brains do not necessarily differentiate between what is real and what we imagine. What's more, when persistent visualisation takes place, the brain adapts itself, preparing our bodies to physically act in a way that's consistent with the imagined event.[65]

Athletes use this technique to great effect in competitive sport. Visualisation raises athletic performance through improved concentration, motivation, coordination, and reduced anxiety.

Fortunately, we don't all need to be professional athletes to benefit from visualisation. The principle can be applied to any type of goal.

Outcome visualisation

Find yourself a quiet place. Pick up your written career goals. Start with the goal most important to you. Whatever it may be, visualise yourself attaining it. Visualise how you will feel, who you will tell, what you will do next. Visualise the sensation of holding that good news letter in your hand, or opening that email. Visualise the accounts showing that your new business has achieved your target income. Visualise the peace and productivity that come with working in your ideal work environment, or the independence and freedom you feel from being self-employed. Imagine the type of person you have become and how you've changed your life for the better.

Keep these images in your mind for as long as possible. Revisit this exercise regularly.

Process visualisation

Go back to your written plan and review the items necessary to execute it. Visualise yourself doing these tasks comfortably and effortlessly each day; visualise how good you'll feel after each one, knowing you're one step closer to your goals and making steady progress. Think about how this newfound productivity may help in other areas of your life. Imagine any obstacles that may come up from time to time, and plan what you'll do to navigate around them.

Visualisation doesn't need to be a time-consuming process. Just a few minutes each day is enough to make a big difference. But it does need to be focused and to include as much detail as possible. Imagining sounds and physical sensations as well as images makes the process even more effective. Make it another new habit, perhaps during the quiet moments at the beginning or end of the day. The more you visualise—and the more detail you include—the easier it will become and the more prepared your brain will be for the actions required to achieve the changes you want.

Avoid negativity

When setting goals, avoid negative drivers for change. This is the difference between *approach goals* (the desire to attain something positive and pleasurable) and *avoidance goals* (the desire to avoid something negative and unpleasant). For example, this is an approach goal: 'I want to change career and work in accordance with my values and skills, by retraining in healthcare and helping others improve their health.' On the other hand, an avoidance goal might be: 'I want to change career because my current role is not in line with my values and I don't feel I'm making a difference to anyone.'

Avoidance goals are harder to specify and less likely to be SMART. This is because they are fuelled by our desire to avoid pain. Avoidance of pain is usually the easier option, but not necessarily the *right* one. When the aim is simply to get out quick, this can lead to repetitive, generic job hunting for anything but the status quo. You may be well-motivated and end up achieving such a goal, but then what? If your only motivation for career change is escaping a bad situation, how do you know the next situation will be any better for you? By contrast, approach goals formulated on a background of self-awareness and focused desire to reach a specific goal are far more life-enriching, confidence-building, and sustainable.

Address limiting self-beliefs

Beliefs are essentially the patterns of thought that we develop. They can be divided into *explicit* and *implicit* beliefs. Explicit beliefs are the things we declare out loud

161

and that we can talk about with ease—they're what we say we believe we can do. However, they do not drive our habits and behaviours. Implicit beliefs are automatic responses based on our inner selves; they're the things we think about ourselves but wouldn't necessarily admit out loud.

It is implicit beliefs that have the power to drive our behaviours. Beliefs and habits are intimately connected, so in this sense, positive implicit self-beliefs have the power to bring about the achievement of goals, while negative implicit self-beliefs can act as barriers. The problem with negative implicit beliefs is that they are not necessarily grounded in reality.

Our self-beliefs are a product of our personality, education, knowledge, and life experiences. Together with our emotional states, they form our self-esteem. We adapt our daily habits and behaviours accordingly and often set up a self-fulfilling prophecy. For example, a student who's told they are no good at maths in school may develop a negative self-belief, lose motivation, avoid the necessary work, and eventually become unable to build on their numeracy skills. They may develop and maintain doubts about their abilities, which are 'confirmed' when they do badly in exams. Later in life, they may find that one of their goals requires knowledge of the subject—perhaps it's a position in finance or sales, or a job that requires further study. They create SMART goals and develop a plan; they develop a good daily habit of disciplined work and study. But they fail to reach their goal. They go through the motions but deep down, they don't believe they'll achieve their goal, because subconsciously they feel they're just not good enough. Their plan and system are flawed right from the start.

Success has less to with raw talent or natural ability than it has to do with sheer grit and perseverance. It requires the ability to fail repeatedly but retain the belief that you are worthy of your goal. If you allow yourself to be limited by negative self-beliefs, you're likely to self-sabotage, to withdraw the effort, consciously or subconsciously. It's easier to admit defeat when you don't put in much effort.

But if beliefs are just patterns of thought, that means

it's possible to change them. So, what can we do about negative self-beliefs?

Positive affirmations for development of positive self-belief

Affirmations are positive statements. The idea is that if you repeat them to yourself daily, you'll create a visualisation of what you want, to transfer it from the conscious to the subconscious mind. Affirmations can help create positive implicit self-beliefs.

Affirmations were popularised in the 1920s by the French Psychologist Emile Coué, and at the time they were known as 'optimistic autosuggestion'. Interestingly, Coué himself went through a career change and only became a psychologist later in life, aged 54. Although he began to study psychology aged 29, he worked as a pharmacist for 28 years before making the switch. His work in psychology was conducted during his retirement. His approach evolved over years of accumulated knowledge and clinical experience, culminating in what became known as *la méthode Coué*.

The Coué Method's mantra has become more famous than the man himself: '*Tous les jours, à tous points de vue, je vais de mieux en mieux* (Every day, in every way, I'm getting better and better).'[66] Coué argued that it was the subconscious mind, not conscious willpower, that held the key to achieving goals and successes in life. In other words, it doesn't matter what you tell yourself, if your subconscious mind doesn't intrinsically believe it. Coué believed that the only way to begin to change subconscious thought patterns—or involuntary 'spontaneous suggestion' as he described it—was through imagination. This was where the beauty of affirmations came into play. They allowed people permission to *imagine* the possibility of a different way of being, and over time, to change their intrinsic self-beliefs.

Coué's method came with some underlying principles:

The affirmation must be believable to the subconscious mind.

So for example, rather than stating, 'I am . . .' you might state, 'I choose to be . . .' Repeatedly telling yourself, 'I am excellent at maths,' will do no good if you implicitly believe you're not. But saying, 'I choose to improve my maths and each day I am getting better at it,' over time, is likely to make a difference.

The conscious mind must accept the affirmation.

This means you need to avoid actively refuting a positive affirmation. Contradictory negative views could actually be counterproductive. Coué argued that the best way to do this was by observing the negative contradictory thought and replacing it with a more positive one.

For example, the affirmation, 'I will give of my best and succeed in my exams,' might be countered by the conscious thought, 'But I can't remember *Theory X*.' So, acknowledge the thought, then say to yourself, 'It will come back to me,' or, 'I can easily revise it.'

Focus on the imagination rather than the conscious will.

Coué described the inner battle between conscious and subconscious as 'self-conflict'. Say, for instance, that your plan involves studying, and this means you need to develop a system of one to two hours of study per day. You may say to yourself, 'I must do this each day otherwise I won't reach my goal,' but you find that the more you try, the harder it is to achieve. So, stop actively trying. The problem with *consciously* trying too hard is that it's exhausting and extrinsically—rather than intrinsically—motivated. Choose to focus on the imaginative affirmation instead: repeat, 'I choose to enjoy spending quiet time studying in my favourite place; more and more each day, it brings me a sense of peace and accomplishment.'

The effects of affirmations have been widely documented anecdotally, and to a lesser extent, empirically. A recent study at Carnegie Mellon University[67] demonstrated that the use of positive affirmations may help improve problem-solving performance under situations of chronic stress. Earlier work by Canadian Researcher Joanne Wood[68] noted that the effect of some types of affirmations may be linked to a person's original self-esteem, with more positive effects apparent when the affirmation is congruent with the person's self-beliefs—which is in line with Coué's original principle.

As with most topics that dare to delve into the workings of our minds, there is so much still unknown and yet to be discovered. Attempts at empirical evidence are often flawed and limited by our complex natures. Only you can know what works for you.

Find yourself a quiet moment and revisit your goals. Look at your plans and the systems you have in place for executing them. Now, observe any negative self-talk that enters your mind as you read each task or goal and write down five affirmations that refute that self-talk, using the principles outlined above. Keep what you've written and get into the habit of revisiting these affirmations every day, perhaps for five minutes first thing in the morning or last thing at night. Note any changes in the way you see yourself or the way you feel in response to certain challenges and situations.

Hold yourself accountable

If you share your goals with others, you are more likely to achieve them. Sharing your goals forces you to commit to them, despite setbacks, which are inevitable. Such setbacks can pop up in various guises—difficulty making plans, logistics of learning new skills, relationship issues, financial worries, even the discovery that your ideal job isn't so ideal after all—but it is human and entirely normal to encounter unexpected twists along the way. This is where it helps to have someone who is aware of your journey and who can hold you accountable.

Being accountable to someone doesn't mean they should tell you off every time you feel like quitting. Instead, they should hold you responsible for the *achievement* of your goals. 'Accountability partners' act as mentors during your journey. They are there to give honest feedback, encouragement, and motivation. To do this, they need to know your clearly-defined goals and detailed plans, so they can help track your progress, celebrate milestones, and ask you questions if they feel you're getting off track. Your accountability partner could be anyone; a work colleague, mentor, family member, friend, or even someone you know who has been through a career change themselves. It could also be a life coach, or someone in a careers group.

Once you've found an accountability partner, check in with them regularly, ideally each week, even if only for ten minutes. It could be in-person or over the phone/Skype. A conversation of some sort is better than email for the generation and flow of ideas, but either way, it needs to be regular. Remember, it's forming the habit that matters.

You may feel you don't need others for accountability because you can track your own progress. The problem with this is that it's in our nature to take the easy road. We procrastinate. If things are getting tough and nobody else knows about our goal, it's easy to put it to one side for a while. But sometimes 'a while' turns into forever. We can pretend our goals never existed in the first place if nobody else knows about them. Accountability partners hold us to our commitments.

What's more, accountability partners can offer more than just accountability. Brainstorming becomes much more productive with two heads together. We all approach problems differently, so having another viewpoint can be invaluable. Your accountability partner may also be able to offer new ideas and help you to overcome barriers. Most importantly, they will be there to give you motivation and encouragement. None of us can achieve our goals alone. Sometimes a little encouragement, at just the right moment, means everything.

Chapter 10

Make It Happen!

*'The journey of a thousand miles
beings with a single step.'*

-LAO TZU

We all have the ability to set amazing goals, but many set them only to never see them through to fruition. Why is this?

The answer lies in habits and behaviours. We don't always have the means to the end. Once the written goals are set, we need to know three things:

1. What to do—a strategy

Once your goal is set, you need to develop a strategy for how to get there.

Let's go back to an earlier example. Remember our hypothetical marketing employee from the SMART goals section of Chapter 9? She wants to gain specialist online marketing skills to set up a small freelancing business. The strategy is to enrol on a course offering those skills, finish it by the end of the year, and begin putting those skills into practice.

2. How to do it—a plan

First, she needs to research available courses and select the most suitable for her budget. She needs to qualify for admission and ensure she plans her working day to manage class attendance, assignment completion, and undertake the necessary daily practice.

3. How to execute the plan—a system

Finally, she needs to develop the habit of studying—and stick at it. It doesn't need to be much—perhaps an hour dedicated to the course at the beginning or end of each working day. Habit allows us to gain mastery over what we do and build the confidence necessary for achievement. Most people are unable to achieve their goals because they underestimate the importance of habit. They direct all their energy and focus into the strategy and plan, and none into the habits required to achieve it. They assume that once the plan is in place, the habits will follow.

Formulating goals and plans are essentially imaginative exercises. While it is important that goals are written down and regularly visualised in the mind, the focus of physical energy needs to be directed totally at habits. You need to change an aspect of your daily routine and this can be hard, particularly if your routines are longstanding. We are wired to avoid pain and seek the familiar, but it is our habits that drive our daily behaviours. And our behaviours dictate our eventual achievements.

Our marketing employee's goal is to run her own business. She plans to prepare and train for this. But it is the focused discipline and daily habits she develops that will dictate her ability to do it all: regular study, taking on feedback and adjusting accordingly, fine-tuning her approach, eating the right foods each day, paying attention to sleep. Sticking to this daily ritual with grit and determination, no matter what.

The same principle applies to any goal. We may not all be aiming for the same things, but the habits, behaviours, and discipline can be applied to our own plans. For major change to happen, we need to make small changes each day such that our new behaviour eventually becomes a habit.

Recognise the power of habits

Changing your habits is crucial to reaching your goals and it requires an understanding of the triggers and rewards that you associate with them. For example, you may habitually have a drink after work. In this case, the trigger might be stress, and the reward might be a sense of calm and relaxation. This is known as positive reinforcement—you repeat the behaviour because you associate it with a pleasurable reward.

Once you can clearly identify the triggers as they happen, you can start to change what you do to achieve the reward. Rather than going for a drink in response to stress, you could try going for a short walk or a gentle run. You will likely feel just as rested and calm afterwards. Your subconscious will come to associate walking or running with a positive reward. Repeat it enough times and you've replaced your old habit with a much better one. What's more, once a behaviour becomes a habit, it requires relatively little motivation to maintain, which highlights the importance of not allowing yourself to be daunted by the prospect of lifelong change. You just need to make a small start, repeat it the next day, and simply keep going.

Sometimes, understanding the trigger is the tricky part. Emotional triggers can go much deeper than just feeling tense or being in pain. If you're having trouble identifying exactly what a trigger is, recognising that the trigger is looming may be enough. Take note and pause before acting. Try it a few times. It is powerful.

What now?

Hopefully, by now you will have set some short-term and long-term goals. You'll have a greater understanding of how you got here and you'll be able to draw on your values and skills to formulate a clearer sense of the type of work that will bring out the best in you. You'll have strategies and plans in place, and you'll have developed a system of working that will bring your plans to fruition. You'll have acknowledged, and started to tackle, any self-limiting beliefs that may have previously held you back. And you'll have shared your goals with an accountability partner, as well as others who will support you along the way.

In terms of self-knowledge, direction, and purpose, you have already achieved more than most do in a lifetime. You are in an excellent position to make well-informed decisions and changes that will lead to self-discovery, growth, and fulfilment. You have set off on the path to a life that is more meaningful for you. You are in a great place. So, what now?

Now you have the blueprint, follow it with confidence. Remind yourself that you have put in the groundwork and you have all the tools you need to navigate your path. Take the time each day to enjoy the *now*. Keep your written goals someplace where you can see them. Spend five minutes each day visualising them. Visualise not just the images, but the sensations and emotions that you will feel as you attain them. Check in with your accountability partner regularly—no less than once a month. This ensures you can review your progress against your plans. Check that you're meeting the short-term deadlines and discuss any barriers you're facing. Allow yourself to take on board any suggestions you receive. Celebrate *all* milestones along the way. The more you do this, the more self-efficacy you will develop.

Don't be afraid to just make a start. The smallest of steps is still a start. Things don't need to begin perfectly; they just need to *begin*. The more momentum you gain, the more you will be able to navigate your way with clarity. Be guided by your plans but don't be afraid to make adjustments along the way—all journeys involve a change of course at some point and changes can lead to new opportunities and experiences. It may be that you need to change the timescale, or perhaps you need to add in more training or more work experience 'tasters'. Perhaps you'll realise as time goes on that you've changed as a person and so have your needs. That's okay. Nothing is static. The more time it takes for you to transition into a new career, the more likely you will be to have different needs by the time you get there. If you're the type of person that needs opportunity for growth and development *now*, the chances are you always will be.

Keep your broad goals in mind as a target, but don't worry if the specifics don't pan out when the time comes. Remember that you are aiming to find something that fits your values, skills, and work environment needs. You're not aiming for a specific title or role because if you do, and then find the work involved is not for you, you may find yourself right back where you started. Allowing labels of any sort to dictate your life course can only lead to disillusionment. Don't feel deflated if things don't turn out quite as you'd planned. Remember that no knowledge or experience is ever wasted. Whatever it is you're aiming for, as long as you stay true to yourself you will reach your true goals.

Do remember to take care of your health. Without this, everything is a struggle. Health matters and prevention is better than cure. Pay daily attention to good nutrition, hydration, exercise, sleep, stress management, and supportive relationships. Keep others in the loop. Share any issues with someone you trust, who can give you an objective viewpoint.

Don't forget that the downsides to staying put can sometimes be far greater than those of making a change. Therefore, be prepared to sacrifice something. Accept that there will be a temporary trade-off in getting to where you want to be. Change isn't always comfortable, but if it's important for your long-term wellbeing, it's worth it.

Remember that obstacles are inevitable. Don't let them get the better of you. Instead, try to anticipate them and have strategies prepared for managing them. Don't be afraid to ask others for advice when it comes to unexpected barriers, whether logistical or emotional;

there are plenty of careers advisers and councillors who specialise in just this. Someone who has already gone through a career change can also help with tips and strategies for tackling obstacles.

Finally, learn to love uncertainty. You never know when or where the next opportunity or idea may come from. The more you open your eyes to the possibility of change, the more opportunities will come your way. Don't be afraid to follow your own star. Know what makes you unique. You have something good and meaningful to offer the world and your challenge is to find a way of doing just that.

> *'Not I, nor anyone else can travel that road for you. You must travel it by yourself. It is not far. It is within reach. Perhaps you have been on it since you were born, and did not know. Perhaps it is everywhere…'*

> *-WALT WHITMAN*

About the Author

Dr Rebecca Healey

MBBS, MSc

Rebecca left a decade-long career as a city-based management accountant in her early thirties. She went on to train in medicine, qualifying as a doctor in 2016. She has since worked in a number of NHS hospital settings in the North of England, additionally setting up her own functional medicine practice, RJ Health & Wellbeing. A self-proclaimed introvert, Rebecca was inspired to write by the recurring challenges experienced across two distinctly different industries, and the strategies she adopted to overcome them. She continues to write regularly on topics related to health and wellbeing, stress management, and nutritional medicine.

Did this book help you?

Reviews are immensely valuable for writers and readers. If you enjoyed this book, please do help spread the word by leaving a review on Amazon. Thank you!

Appendix

Consider the following statements in relation to how you have felt at work in the past month:[69]

1. I look forward to going to work on Monday morning.
2. I feel positive and 'up' most of the time I am working.
3. I have energy at the end of each workday to attend to the people I care about.
4. I have energy at the end of each workday to engage in personal interests.
5. I have the time and energy in my life to read books that interest me.
6. Most interactions at work are positive.
7. I have good friends at work.

8. I feel valued and affirmed at work.

9. I feel recognised and appreciated at work.

10. Work is a real plus in my life.

11. I'm engaged in meaningful work.

12. I feel free to be who I am at work.

13. I feel free to do the things the way I like at work.

14. My values fit with the organisational values.

15. I am aligned with the organisational mission.

16. I trust our leadership team.

17. I respect the work of my peers.

18. I have opportunities to learn what I want to learn.

19. I feel involved in decisions that affect our organisational community.

20. Creativity and innovation are supported.

21. I feel informed about what's going on.

22. I know what is expected of me.

23. I have the materials and equipment that I need to do my work right.

24. I have the opportunity to do what I do best every day at work.

25. My manager cares about me as a person.

26. I know someone at work who encourages my development.

27. My opinions count.

28. My co-workers are committed to doing quality work.

29. My manager reviews my progress.

30. I am fairly compensated.

Bibliography

Acevedo, Bianca P., Elaine N. Aron, Arthur Aron, Matthew-Donald Sangster, Nancy Collins, and Lucy L. Brown. "The highly sensitive brain: an fMRI study of sensory processing sensitivity and response to others' emotions," Brain and Behaviour 4, no.4 (2014): 580-594.

American Psychological Association. "*DSM–5*: Frequently Asked Questions." Accessed May 31, 2020. https://www.psychiatry.org/psychiatrists/practice/dsm/fe edback-and-questions/frequently-asked-questions

American Psychological Association. "Personality." Accessed May 30, 2020. http://www.apa.org/topics/personality/

American Psychological Association. *Stress in America 2017 Snapshot: Coping with Change*. (2017). https://www.apa.org/news/press/releases/stress/2016/cop ing-with-change.pdf

Antonioni, David. (1998). "Relationship between the big five personality factors and conflict management styles." *International Journal of Conflict Management* 9, no.4 (1998): 336-355.

Ariga, Atsunori, and Alejandro Lleras. "Brief and rare mental "breaks" keep you focused: Deactivation and reactivation of task goals pre-empt vigilance decrements. *Cognition* 118 (2011): 439-443.

Aron, Elaine N. Aron. *The Highly Sensitive Person.* London: Thorsons, 2017.

Association of Teachers and Lecturers. "Culture of education targets does little to improve students' grades, but stresses out students and staff." Accessed August 24, 2017.
https://www.atl.org.uk/latest/press-release/culture-education-targets-does-little-improve-students-grades-stresses-out

Barrick, Murray R., Mickael K. Mount, and Timothy A. Judge. "Personality and Performance at the Beginning of the New Millenium: What Do We Know and Where Do We Go Next?" *International Journal of Selection and Assessment* 9, no. 1/2 (2001): 9-30.

Bayne, Rowan. *The Myers-Briggs Type Indicator – A Critical Review and Practical Guide*. London: Chapman & Hall, 1995.

Berns, Gregory S., Jonathan Chappelow, Caroline F. Zink, Guiseppe Pagnoni, Megan E. Martin-Skurski, Jim Richards. "Neurobiological Correlates of Social Conformity and Independence During Mental Rotation." *Society of Biological Psychiatry* 58, no.3 (2005): 245-253.

Bloom, Nicholas, James Liang, John Roberts, and Zhichun Jenny Ying. "Does working from home work? Evidence from a Chinese Experiment." *The Quarterly Journal of Economics* (2015): 165-218.

Boeree, C. George. "Early Medicine and Physiology." (2002).
http://webspace.ship.edu/cgboer/neurophysio.html

Brennan, Aoife, Chugh S. Jasdeep, and Theresa Kline. "Traditional versus open office design: A Longitudinal Field Study." *Environment and Behaviour* 34, no.3 (2002): 279-299.

Briggs Myers, Isabel, and Peter B. Myers. *Gifts Differing: Understanding Personality Type*. 2nd ed. Mountain View: Davies-Black, 2010.

Burns David D. *Feeling Good: The New Mood Therapy.* Reprint ed. New York: Harper-Collins, 2012.

Cain, Susan. *Quiet: The Power of Introverts in a World That Can't Stop Talking.* New York: Broadway Books, 2013.

Cayton, Karuna. *The Misleading Mind: How We Create Our Own Problems and How Buddhist Psychology Can Help Us Solve Them.* Novato: New World Library, 2012.

Centre for Applications of Psychological Type. "Estimated Frequencies of the Types in the United States Population." (2003). https://www.capt.org/products/examples/20025HO.pdf

Cheng, Yawen, Ichiro Kawachi, Eugenie H. Coakley, Joel Schwartz, and Graham Colditz. "Association between psychosocial work characteristics and health functioning in American women: prospective study." *British Medical Journal* 320 (2000): 1432- 1436.

Coue, Emile. *Self mastery through conscious autosuggestion.* Abingdon: Routledge, 2018

Creswell, David J., Janine M. Butcher, William M. P. Klein, Peter R. Harris, John M. Levine. "Self-Affirmation

Improves Problem-Solving under Stress." *PLoS One* 8, no.5 (2013): e62593.

Eurich, Tasha. *Insight: The Power of Self-Awareness in a Self-Deluded World*. London: Macmillan, 2017.

European Commission. "Duration of working life - statistics." Accessed June 10, 2020. https://ec.europa.eu/eurostat/statistics-explained/index.php/Duration_of_working_life_-_statistics

Eysenck, Hans J. *The biological basis of personality*. Oxford: Routledge, 2017.

Eysenck, Hans J. *A model for personality*. New York: Springer, 1981.

Feist, Jess, and Gregory J. Feist. *Theories of Personality*, 8th ed. New York: McGraw-Hill, 2012.

Fishman, Inna, Rowena Ng, and Ursula Bellugi. "Do extraverts process social stimuli differently from introverts?" *Cognitive Neuroscience* 2, no. 2 (2011): 67-73.

Gallagher, Dennis J. "Extraversion, neuroticism and appraisal of stressful academic events." *Personality and Individual Differences* 11, no.10 (1990): 1053-1057.

Gallup. *State of the American Workplace.* (2017). https://cloc.umd.edu/library/research/State%20of%20the%20American%20Workplace%202017.pdf

Gallup. *State of the Global Workplace.* (2013). https://www.gallup.com/workplace/257552/state-global-workplace-2013.aspx

Gallup. *State of the Global Workplace.* (2017). https://www.gallup.com/workplace/238079/state-global-workplace-2017.aspx

Goodhart, Charles Albert Eric. *Monetary Theory and Practice: The U.K. Experience.* New York: Macmillan, 1983.

Inceoglu, Ilke and Peter Warr. "Personality and Job Engagement." *Journal of Personnel Psychology* 10, no.4 (2011): 177-181.

Iroegbu, Manasseh N. "Personality and gender: A Meta-Analysis of Their Effects on Employee Stress." *Global Journal of Interdisciplinary Social Sciences* 3, no.6 (2014): 63-65.

Judge, Timothy A., Daniel Heller, and Michael K. Mount. "Five-factor model of personality and job satisfaction: A meta-analysis." *Journal of Applied Psychology* 87, no. 3 (2002): 530-541.

Jung, Carl Gustav. "Psychological Types, " *Collected Works of C.G. Jung., Vol 6.* Princeton, New Jersey: Princeton University Press, 1971.

Kamimori, G.H., D. M. Penetar, D. B. Headley, D. R. Thorne, R. Otterstetter, and G. Belenky. "Effect of three caffeine doses on plasma catecholamines and alertness during prolonged wakefulness." *European Journal of Clinical Pharmacology* 56 (2000): 537-544.

Kim, Jungsoo, and Richard de Dear. "Workplace satisfaction: The privacy-communication trade-off in open-plan offices." *Journal of Environmental Psychology* 36 (2013): 18-26.

Kumari, Veena, Dominic H. ffytche, Steven C.R. Williams, and Jeffrey A. Gray. (2004). "Personality Predicts Brain Responses to Cognitive Demands." *The Journal of Neuroscience* 24, no. 47 (2004): 10636-10641.

Lally, Phillippa, Cornelia H. M. van Jaarsveld, Henry W. W. Potts, and Jane Wardle. "How are habits formed:

Modelling habit formation in the real world." *European Journal of Social Psychology* 40, no.6 (2010): 998-1009.

Lambert, Nathaniel M., Frank D. Fincham, and Tyler F. Stillman. "Gratitude and depressive symptoms: The role of positive reframing and positive emotion." *Cognition and Emotion* 26, no.4 (2012): 615-633.

Lane, James D., Alison Adcock, Redford B. Williams, and Cynthia M. Kuhn. "Caffeine Effects on Cardiovascular and Neuroendocrine Responses to Acute Psychosocial Stress and Their Relationship to Level of Habitual Caffeine Consumption." *Psychosomatic Medicine* 52, no.3 (1990): 320-336.

Langelaan, Saar, Arnold B. Bakker, Lorenz J.P. va Doornen, and Wilmar B. Schaufeli. "Burnout and work engagement: Do individual differences make a difference?" *Personality and Individual Differences* 40 (2006): 521-532.

Largo-Wright, Erin, W. William Chen, Virginia Dodd, and Robert Weiler. "Healthy Workplaces: The Effects of Nature Contact at Work on Employee Stress and Health." *Public Health Reports* 126, Suppl. 1 (2011): 124-126.

Lazarus, Richard S., and Susan Folkman. "Transactional theory and research on emotions and coping." *European Journal of Personality* 1, no.3 (1987): 141-169.

Lovallo, William R., Niha H. Farag, Andrea S. Vincent, Terrie L. Thomas, and Michael F. Wilson. "Cortisol responses to mental stress, exercise, and meals following caffeine intake in men and women." *Pharmacology, Biochemistry and Behaviour* 83 (2006): 441-447.

Martins, Daniela Canella, Maria Louzada, and Diana Parra. "NOVA. The Star Shines bright." *World Nutrition Journal* 7, no.1-3 (2016), 28-38.

Maruta T., R. C. Colligan, M. Malinchoc, and K. P. Offord. "Optimists vs Pessimists: Survival Rate Among Medical Patients Over a 30 Year Period." *Mayo Clinic Proceedings* 75, no.2 (2000): 140-143.

Maslow, Abraham H. *A Theory of Human Motivation*. Minneapolis: Martino Publishing, 2013.

MBTI Online (2017). *The Complete and Official Guide to Extraversion and Introversion*. (2017). https://www.mbtionline.com/en-US/Articles/2017/June/The-Complete-and-Official-Guide-to-Extraversion--Introversion-eBook

McManus I.C., A. Keeling, and E. Paice. "Stress, burnout and doctors' attitudes to work are determined by personality and learning style: A twelve year longitudinal study of UK medical graduates. *BMC Medicine* 2 (2004): 29.

Meister, I. G., T. Krings, H. Foltys, B. Boroojerdi, M. Muller, R. Topper, and A. Thron. "Playing piano in the mind – an fRMI study on music imagery and performance in pianists." *Cognitive Brain Research* 19 (2004): 219-228.

Mills, Joan, Daniel Robey, and Larry Smith. "Conflict-handling and personality dimensions of project-management personnel." *Psychological Reports* 57 (1985): 1135-1143.

Monteiro, Carlos A., Geoffrey Cannon, Renata Levy, Jean-Claude Moubarac, Patricia Jaime, Ana Paula

NICE. *Mental wellbeing at work*. Public health guideline. (2009). https://www.nice.org.uk/guidance/ph22/resources/mental -wellbeing-at-work-1996233648325

Pannapacker, Wiliam. "Screening Out the Introverts." *The Chronicle of Higher Education* (2012).

http://www.chronicle.com/article/Screening-Out-the-Introverts/131520

Pascual-Leone, Alvaro, Amir Amedi, Felipe Fregni, and Lfti B. Marabet. "The Plastic Human Brain Cortex." *Annual Review of Neuroscience.* 28 (2005): 377-401.

Penley, Julie A., and Joe Tomaka. "Associations among the Big Five, emotional responses, and coping with acute stress." *Personality and Individual Differences* 32 (2002): 1215-1228.

Schwartz, Barry. *Why we work.* London: Simon & Schuster, 2015.

Soderstrom, Marie, Kerstin Jeding, Mirjam Ekstedt, and Aleksander Perski. "Insufficient Sleep Predicts Clinical Burnout." *Journal of Occupational Health Psychology* 17, no.2 (2012): 175-183.

Stephens-Craig, Dana, Matthew Kuofie, and Richard Dool. "Perception of Introverted Leaders by Mid to High-Level Leaders." *Journal of Marketing and Management*, 6, no. 1 (2015): 62-75.

The British Heart Foundation. "Am I drinking too much caffeine?" Accessed June 6, 2020. https://www.bhf.org.uk/informationsupport/heart-matters-magazine/nutrition/ask-the-expert/how-much-caffeine

The Myers & Briggs Foundation. "Isabel Briggs Myers." Accessed May 31, 2020. http://www.myersbriggs.org/my-mbti-personality-type/mbti-basics/isabel-briggs-myers.htm

Tiggemann, Marika, Anthony H. Winefield, and John Brebner. "The role of extraversion in the development of learned helplessness." *Personality and Individual Differences* 3, no.1 (1982): 27-34.

Trade Union Congress. "Workplace stress at record levels, say union health and safety reps." Last modified October 10, 2016. https://www.tuc.org.uk/workplace-issues/health-and-safety/workplace-stress-record-levels-say-union-health-and-safety-reps

Wellness Council of America. *Job Satisfaction Survey.* Accessed June 4, 2020. https://www.welcoa.org/resources/job-satisfaction-survey/

Werner, Kimberley B., Lauren R. Few, and Kathleen K. Bucholz. "Epidemiology, Comorbidity, and Behavioural Genetics of Antisocial Personality Disorder and

Psychopathy." *Psychiatric Annals* 45, no.4 (2015): 195-199.

Wood, Alex M., Stephen Joseph, and John Maltby. "Gratitude uniquely predicts satisfaction with life: Incremental validity above the domains and facets of the five factor model." *Personality and Individual Differences* 45, no.1 (2008): 49-54.

Wood, Joanne V., Elaine Perunovic, and John W. Lee. "Positive self-statements: power for some, peril for others." *Psychological Science* 20, no.7 (2009): 860-866.

Zack, Devora. (2010). *Networking for People who Hate Networking*. San Francisco: Berrett-Koehler, 2010.

Zell, Ethan, and Zlatan Krizan. "Do People Have Insight into Their Abilities? A Metasynthesis." *Perspectives on Psychological Science* 9, no. 2 (2014): 111–125.

Notes

[1] Eurich, *Insight: The Power of Self-Awareness in a Self-Deluded World.*

[2] Zell and Krizan, "Do People Have Insight Into Their Abilities? A Metasynthesis," 111–125.

[3] American Psychological Association, *Personality.* http://www.apa.org/topics/personality/

[4] Feist and Feist, *Theories of Personality.*

[5] C.G. Jung, "Psychological Types."

[6] C. George Boeree, "Early Medicine and Physiology." http://webspace.ship.edu/cgboer/neurophysio.html

[7] *DSM-5: The Diagnostic and Statistical Manual of Mental Disorders.* Handbook used by healthcare professionals in the diagnosis of mental disorders.

[8] D. Zack, *Networking for People who Hate Networking.*

[9] Fishman et al, "Do extraverts process social stimuli differently from introverts?" 67-73.

[10] R. Bayne, *The Myers-Briggs Type Indicator—A Critical Review and Practical Guide.*

[11] Centre for Applications of Psychological Type, "Estimated Frequencies of the Types in the United States Population." https://www.capt.org/products/examples/20025HO.pdf

[12] C.G. Jung, "Psychological Types."

[13] H.J. Eysenck, *The Biological Basis of Personality.*

[14] H.J. Eysenck, *A Model for Personality.*

[15] E.N. Aron, *The Highly Sensitive Person.*

[16] Kumari et al, "Personality Predicts Brain Responses to Cognitive Demands."

[17] Acevedo et al, "The highly sensitive brain: an fMRI study of sensory processing sensitivity and response to others' emotions," 580-594.

[18] Stephens-Craig et al, "Perception of Introverted Leaders by Mid to High-Level Leaders," 62-75.

[19] The Myers & Briggs Foundation, http://www.myersbriggs.org/my-mbti-personality-type/mbti-basics/isabel-briggs-myers.htm

[20] Briggs Myers and Myers, *Gifts Differing: Understanding Personality Type.*

[21] MBTI Online, *The Complete and Official Guide to Extraversion and Introversion,* https://www.mbtionline.com/en-US/Articles/2017/June/The-Complete-and-Official-Guide-to-Extraversion--Introversion-eBook

[22] Maslow, *A Theory of Human Motivation.*

[23] Gallup, *State of the American Workplace.* https://cloc.umd.edu/library/research/State%20of%20the%20American%20Workplace%202017.pdf

[24] Gallup, *State of the Global Workplace.* https://www.gallup.com/workplace/238079/state-global-workplace-2017.aspx

[25] Gallup, *State of the Global Workplace.* *https://www.gallup.com/workplace/257552/state-global-workplace-2013.aspx*

[26] Schwartz, *Why We Work.*

[27] Goodhart, *Monetary Theory and Practice: The U.K. Experience.*

[28] Association of Teachers and Lecturers, "Culture of education targets does little to improve students' grades, but stresses out students and staff." https://www.atl.org.uk/latest/press-release/culture-education-targets-does-little-improve-students-grades-stresses-out

[29] Cain, *Quiet: The Power of Introverts in a World That Can't Stop Talking.*

[30] Barrick et al, "Personality and Performance at the Beginning of the New Millennium: What Do We Know and Where Do We Go Next?" 9-30.

[31] Kim and de Dear, "Workplace satisfaction: The privacy-communication trade-off in open-plan offices," 18-26.

[32] Brennan et al, "Traditional versus open office design: A Longitudinal Field Study," 279-299.

[33] Antonioni, "Relationship between the big five personality factors and conflict management styles," 336-355; Mills et al, "Conflict-handling and personality dimensions of project-management personnel," 1135-1143.

[34] Bloom et al, "Does working from home work? Evidence from a Chinese Experiment," 165-218.

[35] Inceoglu and Warr, "Personality and Job Engagement," 177-181; Judge et al, "Five-factor model of personality and job

satisfaction: A meta-analysis," 530-541; Langelaan et al, "Burnout and work engagement: Do individual differences make a difference?" 521-532; McManus et al, "Stress, burnout and doctors' attitudes to work are determined by personality and learning style: A twelve year longitudinal study of UK medical graduates," 29.

[36] Berns et al, "Neurobiological Correlates of Social Conformity and Independence During Mental Rotation," 245-253.

[37] Tiggemann et al, "The role of extraversion in the development of learned helplessness," 27-34.

[38] Pannapacker, "Screening Out the Introverts." http://www.chronicle.com/article/Screening-Out-the-Introverts/131520

[39] American Psychological Association, *Stress in America 2017 Snapshot: Coping with Change.* https://www.apa.org/news/press/releases/stress/2016/coping-with-change.pdf

[40] Trades Union Congress, "Workplace stress at record levels, say union health and safety reps." https://www.tuc.org.uk/workplace-issues/health-and-safety/workplace-stress-record-levels-say-union-health-and-safety-reps

[41] NICE, *Mental wellbeing at work.* https://www.nice.org.uk/guidance/ph22/resources/mental-wellbeing-at-work-1996233648325

[42] Cheng et al, "Association between psychosocial work characteristics and health functioning in American women: prospective study," 1432-1436.

[43] Lazarus and Folkman, "Transactional theory and research on emotions and coping," 141-169.

[44] Gallagher, "Extraversion, neuroticism and appraisal of stressful academic events." 1053-1057.

[45] Iroegbu, "Personality and gender: A Meta-Analysis of Their Effects on Employee Stress," 63-65.

[46] Gallagher, "Extraversion, neuroticism and appraisal of stressful academic events," 1053-1057.

[47] Penley and Tomaka, "Associations among the Big Five, emotional responses, and coping with acute stress," 1215-1228.

[48] Monteiro et al, "NOVA. The star shines bright," 28-38.

[49] Largo-Wright et al, "Healthy Workplaces: The Effects of Nature Contact at Work on Employee Stress and Health," 124-126.

[50] Lovallo et al, "Cortisol responses to mental stress, exercise, and meals following caffeine intake in men and women," 441-447.

[51] Kamimori et al, "Effect of three caffeine doses on plasma catecholamines and alertness during prolonged wakefulness," 537-544.

[52] The British Heart Foundation, "Am I drinking too much caffeine?" https://www.bhf.org.uk/informationsupport/heart-matters-magazine/nutrition/ask-the-expert/how-much-caffeine

[53] Soderstrom, "Insufficient Sleep Predicts Clinical Burnout," 175-183.

[54] Werner et al, "Epidemiology, Comorbidity, and Behavioural Genetics of Antisocial Personality Disorder and Psychopathy," 195-199.

[55] Lally et al, "How are habits formed: Modelling habit formation in the real world," 998-1009.

[56] Burns, *Feeling Good: The New Mood Therapy*.

[57] Wood et al, "Gratitude uniquely predicts satisfaction with life: Incremental validity above the domains and facets of the five factor model," 49-54.

[58] Lambert et al, "Gratitude and depressive symptoms: The role of positive reframing and positive emotion," 615-633.

[59] Wood et al, "Gratitude influences sleep through the mechanism of pre-sleep cognitions," 43-48.

[60] Maruta et al, "Optimists vs Pessimists: Survival Rate Among Medical Patients Over a 30 Year Period," 140-143.

[61] Ariga and Lleras, "Brief and rare mental 'breaks' keep you focused: Deactivation and reactivation of task goals pre-empt vigilance decrements," 439-443.

[62] Cayton, *The Misleading Mind: How We Create Our Own Problems and How Buddhist Psychology Can Help Us Solve Them.*

[63] European Commission, "Duration of working life - statistics" https://ec.europa.eu/eurostat/statistics-explained/index.php/Duration_of_working_life_-_statistics

[64] Meister et al, "Playing piano in the mind—an fMRI study on music imagery and performance in pianists," 219-228.

[65] Pascual-Leone et al, "The Plastic Human Brain Cortex," 377-401.

[66] Coue, *Self mastery through conscious autosuggestion*.

[67] Creswell et al, "Self-Affirmation Improves Problem-Solving under Stress," e62593.

[68] Wood et al, "Positive self-statements: power for some, peril for others," 860-866.
[69] Wellness Council of America, *Job Satisfaction Survey.*
https://www.welcoa.org/resources/job-satisfaction-survey/

Printed in Great Britain
by Amazon

54487127R00123